CONTENTS

FOREWORD

by Pati Jinich

Over a dozen years ago, I switched careers from policy analysis to cooking. It turns out that sharing a simple plate of enchiladas allows me to connect, explain, and deliver much more than a hundred policy papers ever could. That's because when we eat a new dish, a special door becomes unlocked, allowing us to understand another culture, its stories and its people, with all our senses—truly, with our entire selves. When we see it, smell it, taste it, feel it (and hopefully want to cook it!), all while learning about what's behind it, a deeper sense of who we are can flourish. That's true not only for those who are tasting the food for the first time, but for those sharing it, too. So there is no doubt about it: Food is one of the best ways to venture into different cultures and build bridges between them.

Through my travelogue–cooking show *Pati's Mexican Table* (now in its twelfth season) and my three bestselling cookbooks, I have spent more than a decade sharing the cuisine, culture, and history of my home country of Mexico with audiences in the United States, my new home. I have always been passionate about breaking myths and misconceptions about who we are and how we connect, so in my most recent docuseries, *La Frontera with Pati Jinich*, I have ventured into exploring and celebrating the rich, diverse, and incredibly tasty food and culture of the US-Mexico borderland communities. The more I learn, the more I realize how little I know, and how much more there is to discover and taste. That is just one of the reasons why I am so fascinated by *The Great American Recipe*!

This brilliant, fun, and heartwarming show opens so many windows into the hearts and homes of families across the United States. Each season, a group of exemplary cooks, along with the talented chef judges and host, share the very best of America's home cooking from coast to coast. With each of these dishes, and the stories they tell, we can see the threads that different people, at different times, from so many different cultures and countries, have woven into the great tapestry of the United States. We get a deep dive into the foods that have given so much *sazón* to this country. *Sazón* translates literally to seasoning or flavor, but it goes even further than that: It is the joy of cooking and having food taste right. And these dishes are full of *sazón*, from the schnitzel and eggplant sandwich that is the hottest bite in Israel today to the classic French croque madame, reimagined as mini quiches; from the beloved Southern homeyness of shrimp and grits to the Middle Eastern flair of lamb kebabs; from saucy enchiladas to messy tagliatelle Bolognese; from matzah ball soup to pho to sancocho. These foods are, one by one, becoming American classics in more than a few homes. The growing diversity in the flavors of the United States enriches not only our tables but our lives.

My language of choice is food, and I believe that the best possible food—the most reliable, the most nurturing, and the most worthwhile—is home cooking. It is the unpretentious, delicious, filling recipes that are part of a family's weekly rotation. It is those dishes that never fail you, that always deliver. It is

our true DNA. *The Great American Recipe* is teaching us who we are and who we are becoming, revealing our evolving country on a shared table, for all to enjoy. And through *The Great American Recipe*, and now this cookbook, we all get an exciting opportunity: We get access to those dishes that have been passed down through generations, that are held in a home cook's mind or scribbled on cherished pieces of paper, that hold families and communities together. We get to enjoy something new, unlocking that special door and finding a delicious new route to greater understanding.

I can't wait to start cooking my way through *The Great American Recipe Cookbook*. And that is not only because I know that it will help me solve many Wednesday night dinner riddles with new flavors and fascinating stories. It is also because I know I will come out of it with more knowledge of and appreciation for who we are today—and *The Great American Recipe* will make my kitchen a more magical place to learn.

Un abrazo,
Pati

INTRODUCTION

Welcome back to *The Great American Recipe Cookbook*! Pull up a chair and get ready to dig into more than one hundred recipes that celebrate the diversity of flavors, authentic cooking styles, and rich stories that make American home cooking so unique—and so heartwarming.

Sharing our most treasured recipes and the stories behind them is what *The Great American Recipe* is all about. The phrase "American food" often brings to mind certain classic dishes: a fried chicken recipe served up at a summer picnic or a honey-glazed ham gracing the table at the holidays. And those meals are delicious ones to celebrate, especially when we can share them with the people we love. But those quintessentially "American" foods represent only a narrow sliver of what our country's cuisine really is. We are one nation with more than one million kitchens, each with its own heritage, culture, and community—making American food an amazing mix of different culinary traditions that bring together flavors from around the country and beyond.

The home cooks who compete on *The Great American Recipe* are perfect examples. Season one of the hit PBS series featured the recipes and culinary legacies of home cooks from the Midwest to Mexico. On the second season, the next batch of amazing home cooks competed over eight weeks to see whose dishes were worthy of the title "Great American Recipe" and to have one of their dishes featured on the cover of this book. Traveling from their homes in Colorado, Florida, Georgia, Hawai'i, Idaho, Illinois, Kansas, New York, and Ohio, this season's cooks brought incredible dishes representing a range of traditions, from the staple meals that immigrant families brought from around the world, to the Indigenous fare that Native Americans have been cooking for generations. Only in America could you find a Shabbat dinner of noodle kugel served alongside Vietnamese pho made with bison for a Native spin! The contestants participated in new challenges and even got a chance to show off their sweet sides at the first Great American Recipe Bake Sale, sharing decadent chocolate brownies, a Hawaiian take on the Japanese cake confection manju, and more. In these pages, we've gathered the most memorable recipes from the show.

Once again, the show and the cookbook owe so much to the host and judges—Alejandra, Tiffany, Leah, and Graham—for their guidance and creativity. As a lifestyle and food contributor and writer, host Alejandra Ramos has created hundreds of recipes that combine the Puerto Rican foods she grew up eating in New York City with the dishes and flavors she's fallen in love with along the way. Tiffany Derry is an award-winning chef whose acclaimed restaurants in Texas celebrate the soul of Southern farm-to-table cooking. Leah Cohen is a celebrated chef, restaurateur, and cookbook author whose cuisine combines classical Western cooking with the robust flavors of her Filipina heritage. Growing up on naval bases around the world, Graham Elliot was exposed to cuisine from every continent. His culinary gift earned his eponymous Chicago restaurant a rare two Michelin stars, and he eventually returned to the Hawai'i of his youth, blending the local flavors of the islands into his inventive cuisine. Look for their new recipes throughout the book as well.

MEET THE COOKS

Abbe Odenwalder

Abbe is a recipe writer, crafts maker, and mother of two who has been living in Denver, Colorado, for forty years. She currently lives with her husband and their Skye terrier, Gordy. She grew

up the oldest of three in Kankakee, Illinois, a small farming and industrial town about an hour south of Chicago. Her parents would regularly take them on trips to Chicago to introduce them to food, art, and culture that they weren't able to experience in their small town. Her grandfather, who immigrated from Lithuania with her father in 1939, was the town butcher, so from an early age Abbe understood the importance of food in people's lives. Abbe started learning to cook while helping her mother in the kitchen as a child, but she really started cooking when she was in college. Abbe was raised observing Jewish traditions, and although she loves to experiment with new ingredients and cuisines, she always goes back to her traditional Jewish recipes for the holidays.

Brad Mahlof

Brad is a real estate developer who lives on the Upper East Side of New York City. He grew up in Deal, New Jersey, a predominantly Syrian Jewish enclave about an hour south of the city with his parents,

twin brother Elliot, and two younger siblings. While they're not Syrian themselves, Brad's dad, who is of Libyan Jewish descent, chose the town because he felt comfortable there after emigrating from Israel.

Brad has been deeply influenced by his ancestors' history and traditions and carries them on through the food he cooks, including keeping kosher. Shabbat, the Jewish Sabbath, is an important part of his week. Whether he's with his family or with friends, the practice of leaving the busyness of the world behind and showing appreciation for what he has is his favorite thing to do and at the core of who he is. Brad's mission is to share with the world the recipes that have been passed down to him, bringing modern sensibility to traditional dishes.

Khela Brewer

Khela Brewer is a next-level midwestern soccer mom: Her husband is a soccer coach and her two sons have grown up in the sport, traveling and competing at higher levels. Khela herself is

no stranger to competition, having entered (and won!) many local cooking competitions. A born-and-raised Kansas City girl, Khela lives to feed the people she loves, and she takes full advantage of the burgeoning foodie scene in her hometown, going to every restaurant and meeting every chef she can. Her family recipes are all-American (Khela's mom was from North Carolina and moved to KC in her twenties, bringing with her the family's cherished chicken and dumplings recipe, which Khela still craves and makes today), but she is so inspired by all of the different cuisines that Kansas City has to offer. Khela may be from the land of meat and potatoes, but she makes a japchae that her friends and family beg for.

Leanna Pierre

Leanna is general counsel for a financial tech firm and lives outside Atlanta with her husband, Jaques, and her (bonus) son, JJ. Leanna was born in the Bronx to parents who both emigrated from Barbados. Her dad came over in his late teens and brought over his childhood sweetheart, Leanna's mom, to join him shortly after. Their family lived in a three-unit building above her uncle and his family on the ground floor and below her grandmother Felis on the top floor. As a child, she used to go upstairs most nights to Felis's apartment, waiting up until she would get home from work just to get a hug good night.

Leanna's cooking is influenced heavily by the Bajan recipes her mom and grandmothers prepared, but she has also been influenced by the melting pot of NYC cuisine, and now, Southern specialties have become part of her repertoire as well. Leanna hopes to dispel the misconception that all Caribbean food is the same by helping people appreciate the nuances.

Maria Givens

Seattle resident Maria was born and grew up in Coeur d'Alene, Idaho, and is a member of the Indigenous tribe of the same name. She owns a consulting business that concentrates on food systems planning and design to assist in Tribal sovereignty, Indigenous DEI training, and cultural education. Her mom is also Coeur d'Alene, and it is from her and other ancestors that Maria learned how to cook starting at a young age.

The Coeur d'Alene believe in the concept of the seven generations: yours, the three before, and the three after. You must honor those who came before and impact the future of those ahead. Maria hopes that by sharing her recipes she can help Native people become closer to their ancestral foods and help non-Indigenous people respect the foods of this land. While she loves to prepare the foods of her ancestors, Maria has also been influenced by the people and places she has lived and incorporates those lessons into her food, as evidenced by her bison pho.

Mike Thomas

Mike is a special education teacher who was born and raised—and is now raising his own three children—in Cleveland, Ohio. He lived in the same house as his grandparents growing up, and once his grandfather passed on, Mike took up the role of helping his grandmother Helen in the kitchen. When he ate his grandma's food, he could feel the love and time she put into it, and he strives to evoke the same emotions with the meals he serves today.

The Thomas family recipes are rooted in Southern cuisine (his grandparents came from Mississippi). Those remain relatively unchanged because he firmly believes you don't mess with the ancestors' recipes. That said, as a proud Clevelander, he embraces the many cultures around him in his community and has become well known for his take on pad thai. Mike hosts a "Sunday Funday" get-together centered around food and family every weekend, and he has a side hustle catering about ten events a month.

Relle Lum

Relle is first and foremost a mom to her two kiddos, Kyten and Kylena. She was born and raised in Maui, Hawai'i, in a tight-knit community where every neighbor is considered family,  and family is everything. A nurse practitioner, Relle likes to care for people through traditional medicine and the "medicine" that comes from eating a good meal. She believes that there is no better feeling than making a dish and having people love it, noting that an 'ono (delicious) meal makes the whole day better. Her specialty is desserts, a skill set (and sweet tooth!) that she inherited from her mother, though she credits her grandmother for teaching her how to cook the meals of their ancestors. Hawai'i is one big melting pot of several different cultures, and Relle has Native Hawaiian, Japanese, Portuguese, Chinese, and African American heritage. Through her blog, Relle loves to share Hawaiian culture and its vast and diverse cuisine with mainland America.

Salmah Hack

Salmah, a first-generation American, was born to two Guyanese immigrants in the "Little Guyana" neighborhood of Richmond Hill, Queens, in New York City. Although she is just a girl  from Queens who now lives in Florida, the food Salmah cooks is the food her parents grew up on, and their parents before them, forever connecting her to where she truly comes from. Salmah was raised in the kitchen, learning and spending time with her mom, grandmother, cousins, and aunties, cooking the traditional foods of their Guyanese and Indian ancestors. These days Salmah is constantly cooking for her friends, her neighbors, her coworkers—anyone she can drop off a cake to—and she comes by that naturally. As a Muslim, she was raised holding charity and compassion to a high standard, and she has raised her two children with the same values, noting that the smallest act of charity is a smile. She is at her happiest when surrounded by her food and her family.

Ted Pappas

Ted is a semiretired architect, home builder, and consultant who lives with his wife and two daughters in a small, close-knit suburb of Chicago. Ted has lived in Chicagoland all his  life and grew up in Edison Park, a neighborhood on the edge of the city where his family owned a small breakfast restaurant. Though he first learned to cook from his mother—he and his sister helped with prep and got fresh ingredients from their garden—he didn't really get into cooking until he went away to college and had to fend for himself.

Ted's cooking is heavily influenced by his Greek heritage (his father was raised in Greece and moved to the US when he was thirty, and all four of his mother's grandparents were born in Greece as well). In Greek culture, and especially in his household, cooking is a way to show affection. He thinks there's nothing more fun than connecting through food, and now his daughters are helping him share his recipes on social media.

Appetizers, Snacks, and Sides

Corn Chaat with Curried Watermelon 3

Baigan Choka and Dhal 4
(Smoked Eggplant with Yellow Split Peas)

Brik 9

Cassava Balls and Mango Sour 11

Fried Plantains 13

**Roasted Sweet Potato
with Candied Pecans** 14

Tershi with Harissa 15

**Roasted Butternut Squash with Sweet
and Sour Onions and Pomegranate** 17

Crab Cakes with Roasted Corn Salsa 19

**Vietnamese Soft-Shell Crab
with Nước Chẩm Sauce** 21

Bajan Fish Cakes 24

Saltfish and Ackee with Fried Dumplings 27

S'feeha and Manakish 28
(Meat and Za'atar Cheese Pies)

**Spam Katsu Musubi and
Mochiko Chicken Musubi** 31

Corn Chaat with Curried Watermelon

KHELA

My dear friend Jyoti has been teaching Indian cooking classes at her home for over twelve years and showed me how to make this fabulous warm-and-cold salad pairing. She is an excellent human who donates the proceeds from her classes to her favorite local charities—and bonus, her food is amazing. That talent is on full display here: A warm roasted corn salad (a traditional Indian dish) is paired with a chilled spiced watermelon salad (a Jyoti original), and both are delicious. I especially like to prepare these in the heat of the summer, when fresh corn and watermelon are plentiful. Something about those ingredients together screams summertime on a plate. **Serves 6**

1. Put the watermelon in a large bowl.

2. In a small nonstick skillet, heat the oil over medium heat. Add the nigella seeds and cook just until they begin to sizzle. Quickly add the coriander and cumin and immediately turn off the heat. Stirring constantly, pour the sizzling mixture over the watermelon. Cover and chill in the refrigerator. Season with salt right before serving.

3. While the watermelon is chilling, make the corn chaat. In a large skillet, heat the oil over medium heat. Add the corn kernels and toss until most are lightly browned, 5–8 minutes. Remove the pan from the heat and stir in the ginger, lemon juice, green chile, and cilantro. Season with salt and pepper. Serve warm, with the chilled watermelon.

Curried watermelon

1 small seedless watermelon, rind removed, cut into bite-size pieces

2 tablespoons vegetable oil

½ teaspoon nigella seeds

¾ teaspoon ground coriander

½ teaspoon ground cumin

Salt to taste

Corn chaat

1 tablespoon vegetable oil

6 ears corn, kernels removed

1 teaspoon finely grated fresh ginger

Juice of 1 lemon

1 small Indian green chile, minced

1½ tablespoons chopped fresh cilantro

Salt and ground black pepper to taste

Baigan Choka and Dhal
Smoked Eggplant with Yellow Split Peas

SALMAH

Garlic-stuffed roasted eggplant, pureed and served with a smooth, warm aromatic lentil dhal . . . it's what Guyanese breakfast dreams are made of! Nothing can compare to being awakened by the smell of the charred eggplant mixed with garlic and the sizzle of the chunkay (tempered garlic and spices) for the dhal. Starting your day with baigan choka and dhal, you know it's off to a good start! **Serves 6**

Baigan choka

2 medium eggplants

9 garlic cloves, thinly sliced

2 Roma tomatoes

2 wiri wiri peppers, finely chopped

1 small yellow onion, chopped

3 tablespoons vegetable oil

3 tablespoons cumin seeds

3 tablespoons salt

2 tablespoons ground black pepper

¼ cup finely chopped fresh cilantro

4 scallions, thinly sliced

Naan or frozen parathas, heated, for serving

Dhal

4 tablespoons vegetable oil, divided

1 medium yellow onion, sliced

7 garlic cloves, 3 minced and 4 thinly sliced

3 wiri wiri peppers, sliced

½ teaspoon ground turmeric

1½ teaspoons salt

1 cup dried yellow split peas, rinsed

4¼ cups water

1 teaspoon cumin seeds

½ teaspoon mustard seeds

1. Using a paring knife, make 4–5 slits in the eggplants. Stuff the garlic slices into the slits.

2. Wrap each eggplant in aluminum foil. Wrap each tomato in aluminum foil.

3. Place the wrapped parcels directly over a medium-low flame on the stovetop or grill. Rotating parcels every 3–5 minutes, char and cook the eggplants for 20 minutes and the tomatoes for 10 minutes. Once soft and juicy, remove from the heat and set aside to cool.

4. While the eggplants and tomatoes cool, make the dhal. Select the sauté mode on an Instant Pot Press and wait 30 seconds for the pot to heat up. Add 2 tablespoons of the oil, the onion, minced garlic, wiri wiri peppers, turmeric, and salt. Sauté until fragrant, 5–6 minutes. Add the split peas and sauté for 3–4 minutes. Press "cancel." Pour in the water. Lock the lid into place and set to sealing. Cook on high pressure for 12 minutes. Release the pressure naturally for 10 minutes, then manually release the remaining pressure, press "cancel," and remove the lid.

5. Using a handheld immersion blender or dhal ghutni (traditional wooden swivel stick), puree the dhal till smooth. Put the lid back on and set aside while you make the chunkay.

6. Heat the remaining 2 tablespoons oil in a small saucepan over low heat. Add the sliced garlic, cumin seeds, and mustard seeds. Fry until the garlic slices have browned and the cumin seeds have darkened. Remove the pan from the heat. With the pan in one hand, remove the Instant Pot lid with the other hand, quickly turn the pan upside down, and pour the mixture over the dhal, then immediately cover the Instant Pot with the lid to allow the dhal to absorb the smoky flavor.

(recipe continues)

7. To finish the baigan choka, unwrap the foil parcels. Cut the eggplants in half and scoop the flesh into a large bowl. Scoop the tomato flesh into the same bowl. Add the wiri wiri peppers and mash till smooth. Add the onion on top but do *not* mix it in.

8. Heat the oil in a small skillet over medium heat. Add the cumin seeds and sizzle until the cumin seeds turn brown, 5–6 minutes. Pour the hot oil and cumin seeds over the onion on top of the eggplant mixture. Let sizzle for 2 minutes, then season with the salt, pepper, and cilantro.

9. To serve, ladle the dhal into each dish. Top with the baigan choka. Garnish with the scallions and serve with naan or paratha.

Brik

BRAD

Brik is a North African dish made from warqa pastry that is filled with a raw egg and then deep-fried, leaving a crispy pastry exterior and a gorgeously runny egg in the center. This traditional street food, one of my favorite treats growing up, is now popular in the Israeli shuk (outdoor market) and beyond. While the pastry takes some practice, it's well worth it and is sure to impress your friends and family! **Makes 12 pastries**

1. To make the warqa batter, in a blender, combine the flour, oil, salt, semolina, and ⅔ cup water and blend until smooth. Check the consistency. If the batter is too thick to spread thinly, add up to ⅓ cup more water and blend again until smooth.

2. Bring a large pot of water to a boil. Place a nonstick skillet on top of the pot of boiling water and lightly grease the skillet. Using a pastry brush, brush the batter in a circular shape in the skillet. Make as many overlapping brush strokes as necessary to create an even circle of batter with no gaps. (Just like crepes, the first one tends to be a sacrificial one. It's a little tricky but becomes easier with practice.)

3. Let the batter cook for about 2 minutes (it will not brown but the top will look dried out), then gently peel the warqa off the pan with a silicone spatula or skewer and place it on a paper towel to cool. Repeat to create 11 more warqas.

4. Pour about 4 inches of oil into a large, heavy pot and heat over medium-high heat to 375 degrees F.

5. To make the dipping sauce, combine the tomatoes, garlic, and salt in a small bowl. Set aside.

6. Crack an egg into an individual prep bowl and sprinkle the top with a pinch of the chopped parsley, scallions, and salt to taste.

7. Lift one warqa gently by the edge and lower it into the hot oil while still holding on to it. Add the cracked egg with parsley and scallions into the center of the warqa and then quickly fold it in half with a metal spatula to seal it into a half-moon shape. Cook until the warqa is golden and the egg is cooked but the yolk is still runny, about 1 minute. Transfer to paper towels to drain briefly. Prepare the remaining brik in the same manner, repeating steps 6 and 7, returning the oil to 375 degrees F between batches.

8. Serve the brik with the dipping sauce and spicy peppers.

Warqa

1⅝ cups all-purpose flour

1 tablespoon vegetable oil

½ teaspoon kosher salt

2 tablespoons coarse semolina

⅔–1 cup room-temperature water

Filling

12 large eggs

2 tablespoons chopped fresh parsley

2 tablespoons chopped scallions

Kosher salt to taste

Dipping sauce

3 Roma tomatoes, grated on the large holes of a box grater

1 garlic clove, grated

1 teaspoon salt, plus more to taste

Frying and serving

Vegetable oil, for frying

Israeli spicy peppers, for garnish

Cassava Balls and Mango Sour

SALMAH

This is a classic Guyanese street food snack: a hard-boiled egg encased in fluffy mashed seasoned cassava, fried, and served with a spicy sour mango sauce. As children, my parents purchased them from street vendors or snackettes on their walk home from school, and when I was growing up, we would buy them from roti shops. I often make this snack for my own children so they can share in the joy and history of this popular street food. **Makes 10 balls**

1. Bring a medium pot of water to a simmer. Gently lower the eggs into the simmering water and cook for 7–8 minutes for a creamy hard-boiled egg. While the eggs are cooking, fill a large bowl with ice-cold water. Using a strainer, transfer the eggs from the simmering water to the ice-cold water. Let cool completely, then drain.

2. Meanwhile, bring a large pot of water to a boil. Add the cassava and cook until tender when pierced with a fork, about 15 minutes. Drain the cassava and transfer to a bowl to cool slightly.

3. When cool enough to handle, remove the vein or fibrous middle section of the cassava pieces and discard. Run the remaining soft cassava through a food mill or mash with a potato masher until smooth. Add the melted butter, salt, pepper, wiri wiri peppers, garlic, culantro, and scallions. Combine until evenly incorporated and smooth.

4. Peel the chilled hard-boiled eggs.

5. Flatten about ¼ cup of the seasoned cassava mixture in the palm of your hand, shaping it into a disk. Add a hard-boiled egg to the center of the disk, then fold and wrap the cassava around the egg, gently rolling it to seal. Repeat until all of the eggs are coated with the cassava mixture.

6. Place the cassava-wrapped eggs in the fridge to chill for about 10 minutes while you get ready to fry them.

7. Heat the oil in a large skillet over medium-high heat to 350–375 degrees F. Set a wire rack over a rimmed baking sheet.

8. In a shallow bowl, whisk together the flour, garlic powder, dried thyme, and salt to taste.

10 large eggs, at room temperature

3 cassavas (about 2 pounds), peeled and cut into 2-inch pieces

2 tablespoons unsalted butter, melted

2 teaspoons salt, plus more for seasoning

2 teaspoons ground black pepper

3 wiri wiri peppers or 1 Scotch bonnet pepper, minced

4 garlic cloves, grated

¼ cup finely chopped fresh culantro, plus more for garnish

3 scallions, thinly sliced

3 cups vegetable oil, for frying

1 cup all-purpose flour

2 teaspoons garlic powder

2 tablespoons dried thyme

(recipe continues)

9. Dredge each cassava-egg ball in the seasoned flour mixture, dusting off any excess flour. Add three or four balls to the oil and fry, turning until golden brown all over, 3–4 minutes per side. Transfer the balls to the wire rack to drain and cool. Repeat to fry all the cassava-egg balls.

10. To serve, spoon some of the sour mango sauce onto each plate. Slice a cassava ball in half and place on the sauce. Garnish with culantro and serve.

№ 2 | Mango Sour

1 large green (unripe) mango, peeled, pitted, and roughly chopped

2½ cups water

5 garlic cloves, chopped

2 hot peppers, seeded and chopped

¼ cup white vinegar

1 tablespoon sugar

Salt to taste

1. Combine all the ingredients in a medium saucepan. Bring the mixture to a boil over medium-low heat, then simmer until the mango has absorbed most of the liquid, about 20 minutes.

2. Using an immersion blender, puree the mixture until smooth and slightly runny.

Fried Plantains

LEANNA

One of the things that makes plantain so great is how versatile it is. It can be fried, boiled, baked, or mashed. It can be eaten for breakfast, lunch, dinner, or even a snack. It can be as sweet as a dessert or as savory as a potato pancake; it all depends on how ripe the plantain is or isn't. To make sweet plantains, you want to make sure you choose plantains that are yellow with some black spots on them. The deeper the shade of yellow and the more black spots there are on the peel, the sweeter the plantain will be. This recipe (and I hesitate to call it a recipe because the plantain really does all of the work) is my favorite way to have plantain. **Serves 6**

1. Pour enough oil into a large skillet to heavily coat the bottom of the pan. Heat the oil over medium-high heat. Working in batches, add the plantain slices to the hot oil. Fry for 2–3 minutes on each side, depending on the desired crispiness. Transfer to a paper towel–lined plate. Season with salt and serve immediately.

Vegetable oil, for frying

2 medium ripe plantains, peeled and cut on the diagonal into ½-inch-thick slices

Salt to taste

Roasted Sweet Potato with Candied Pecans

KHELA

Thanksgiving is my favorite holiday. My husband has joked that it's my Super Bowl. I make a mean spatchcocked, dry-brined turkey, but to be honest, my favorite things at Thanksgiving—other than the time with family—are the sides, especially my sweet potatoes with candied pecan topping. What makes these sweet potatoes different from most is roasting them in the oven first and the addition of orange. Roasting brings out the natural sweetness and keeps the bright color, while the orange gives them that little something extra. **Serves 8**

Sweet potatoes

4 large sweet potatoes

Grated zest of ½ orange

Juice of 1 orange

2 tablespoons heavy cream, or more as needed

2 tablespoons unsalted butter, melted

1 teaspoon salt

½ teaspoon grated nutmeg

Topping

½ cup packed brown sugar

4 tablespoons (½ stick) unsalted butter, melted

1 teaspoon salt

¾ cup pecans, chopped

1. Preheat the oven to 400 degrees F. Lined a rimmed baking sheet with aluminum foil.

2. Using a fork, poke holes all over the sweet potatoes and place them on the prepared baking sheet. Bake for about 45 minutes, until the potatoes are soft and easily pierced with a knife. Let the potatoes cool slightly. Turn the oven down to 375 degrees F.

3. While the potatoes are cooling, prepare the topping. Combine the brown sugar, melted butter, salt, and pecans in a medium bowl. Stir the mixture around until most of the brown sugar has darkened from the butter. Set aside.

4. When the potatoes are cool enough to handle, peel off the skins and put the flesh in a large bowl, breaking it up a bit with your fingers. Add the orange zest and juice, cream, melted butter, salt, and nutmeg. Using an electric hand mixer, blend the potatoes on medium speed until smooth, adding more cream if needed.

5. Lightly grease a small casserole dish. Transfer the potato mixture to the casserole dish, pressing down so it is evenly spread out in the dish. Sprinkle the top with the sugared pecans as evenly as possible, then bake for 15–20 minutes, until the topping is crunchy. Serve warm.

Tershi with Harissa

Tershi is the spicy, tangy, garlicky dip you didn't know you needed. This traditional Libyan Jewish dip made of squash or pumpkin is perfect for a fall treat. It's easy to make and a wonderful condiment to add to anything. **Serves 6**

BRAD

1. Preheat the oven to 400 degrees F.

2. Put the squash and carrots in a 13 × 9-inch baking pan. Drizzle with olive oil and season with salt. Pour about ½ inch water into the baking pan. Cover with aluminum foil and roast for 40 minutes, or until soft.

3. In a food processor, combine the Aleppo pepper, whole garlic clove, vinegar, cumin, coriander, caraway, and salt and puree. Add ¼ cup of the oil and process again until combined.

4. Drain the roasted veggies and transfer to a large bowl. Add the remaining ¼ cup oil, harissa, minced garlic, and lemon juice and mash to combine well. Adjust the seasoning to taste and garnish with the chives.

1 small butternut squash, peeled, seeded, and cubed

2 large carrots, chopped

½ cup olive oil, divided, plus more for drizzling

Kosher salt to taste

½ cup Aleppo pepper

6 garlic cloves, peeled, 1 left whole and 5 minced

1½ tablespoons red wine vinegar

1 teaspoon ground cumin

½ teaspoon ground coriander

½ teaspoon ground caraway

1–2 tablespoons spicy harissa

3 tablespoons lemon juice

Chopped fresh chives, for garnish

Roasted Butternut Squash with Sweet and Sour Onions and Pomegranate

During the fall and winter months, squash is abundant and very accessible. I love butternut squash, and after caramelizing in the oven its natural flavors really sing. Brown butter adds a nuttiness and savory flavor to this dish. Any way I can eat pomegranate seeds, I'm game. This dish can be served on its own, as a side, or for the holidays. It's one of those recipes that's good to keep in your pocket. **Serves 4**

1. Preheat the oven to 400°F. Lightly grease a rimmed baking sheet.

2. Rub the cut sides of the squash with 2 tablespoons of the olive oil and 2 teaspoons of the salt. Place the squash halves, cut side down, on the prepared baking sheet. Bake until fork tender, 45 minutes to 1 hour.

3. Meanwhile, heat the remaining 1 tablespoon olive oil in a small skillet over medium-high heat. Add the onion and remaining 1 teaspoon salt and cook, stirring frequently, until the onion is well softened and darkening, at least 15 minutes. Reduce the heat to medium, and add the vinegar and syrup. Stir and reduce until the mixture is jammy and the onion is broken down, at least another 15 minutes or so. Add the mint and adjust seasoning if need be.

4. Melt the butter in a small saucepan over medium heat, stirring constantly. Keep on stirring and cooking the butter until it turns golden brown and smells nutty, 5–8 minutes. You will see brown specks begin to form at the bottom of the pan; this is OK, but be sure not to let the butter blacken, which means it has burned.

5. Arrange the squash cut side up on a serving platter. Spread with the sweet and sour onions and pour the brown butter into the "cups" of the squash. Sprinkle with the pomegranate seeds and red pepper flakes, scatter the arugula on top, and serve.

1 (1½- to 2-pound) butternut squash, halved lengthwise and seeded

3 tablespoons extra-virgin olive oil, divided

3 teaspoons kosher salt, divided

1 large yellow onion, thinly sliced

¼ cup apple cider vinegar

¼ cup maple syrup

2 tablespoons chopped fresh mint

8 tablespoons (1 stick) unsalted butter

¼ cup pomegranate seeds

½ teaspoon red pepper flakes

1 handful arugula

1 handful microgreens, optional

Crab Cakes with Roasted Corn Salsa

LEANNA

If I order a crab cake, I expect it to be packed with crab, not a bunch of filler, which is why I usually make my own. If you are like me and want your crab cakes to actually taste like crab, not breading, then you have come to the right place. These crab cakes are packed with jumbo crab meat and served with a colorful and vibrant corn salsa that is bound to leave you coming back for more. **Serves 6**

1. Preheat the oven to 375 degrees F.

2. In a medium bowl, combine the crabmeat, onion, bell pepper, chives, and Creole seasoning. Mix the ingredients so that they are evenly distributed throughout the crabmeat. Add the lime juice, eggs, and mayonnaise and stir again until well incorporated. Add the panko and stir one more time, making sure everything is evenly dispersed.

3. Put the butter in a 13 × 9-inch baking dish and melt the butter in the oven; this should take no more than 1–2 minutes. Once the butter has melted, remove the dish from the oven.

4. Take about 2 tablespoons of the crabmeat mixture and pat it into a cake; place the crab cake in the buttered baking dish. Repeat until you have used all the crabmeat mixture.

5. Bake for 15 minutes. Remove the baking dish from the oven and, using a small brush, brush some melted butter from the bottom of the baking dish on top of each crab cake.

6. Bake for another 10 minutes. Using a spatula or butter knife, carefully lift the edges of each crab cake before removing it for plating. This will help ensure that the crab cakes don't break apart.

7. While the crab cakes are baking, stir together the spicy mayo ingredients in a bowl. To serve, scoop some corn salsa (recipe follows) onto each plate and place a crab cake and some spicy mayo alongside.

Crab cakes

6 cups jumbo lump crabmeat, picked over

⅔ cup diced red onion

1 cup diced red bell pepper

½ cup chopped fresh chives

2 tablespoons plus 2 teaspoons Creole seasoning or Old Bay

Juice of 1 lime

4 large eggs, beaten

¼ cup mayonnaise

1 cup panko bread crumbs

4 tablespoons (½ stick) unsalted butter

Spicy mayo

1 cup mayonnaise

2 tablespoons hot sauce

Juice of ½ lime

(recipe continues)

№ 2 | Roasted Corn Salsa

4 ears sweet corn, husks
  and silk removed

1 red onion, diced

3–4 Roma tomatoes,
  chopped

1 bunch cilantro, roughly
  chopped

Kosher salt and ground
  black pepper to taste

Juice of 1–2 limes

1. Preheat a grill to medium-high heat.

2. Grill the ears of corn, turning occasionally, until
    lightly browned, 15–20 minutes.

3. Remove the corn from the grill and set aside to cool
    slightly. Once cool enough to handle, stand each ear
    over a shallow bowl and use a sharp knife to slice the
    corn kernels off the cob.

4. Put the corn kernels in a large bowl and add the
    onion, tomatoes, and cilantro. Stir well to make sure
    everything is nicely combined, then season with salt
    and pepper. Squeeze the lime juice over the salsa just
    before serving.

Vietnamese Soft–Shell Crab with Nước Chấm Sauce

Soft-shell crab was my first introduction to Vietnamese food. Back in the '80s, a small Vietnamese restaurant opened in Denver and we decided we needed to join the line to see what all the fuss was about. As we stood at the pass, platters of fried soft-shell crab passed before our eyes served with green leaf lettuce, fresh herbs, and an amazing spicy-sweet lime-flavored nước chấm dipping sauce. So don't hesitate when you see soft-shell crabs. This splurge is so worth it and these beer-battered crabs are so easy to make! **Serves 6**

(recipe continues)

Crabs

1 cup all-purpose flour

¾ cup cornstarch

2¼ teaspoons baking powder

1½ teaspoons ground turmeric

¾ teaspoon kosher salt

½ teaspoon cayenne pepper

1 large egg

1½ teaspoons rice wine vinegar

6 ounces light wheat beer, or more as needed

Vegetable or peanut oil, for frying

8 jumbo soft-shell crabs, cleaned

To serve

Leaf lettuce

Fresh cilantro leaves

Fresh mint leaves

Fresh Thai basil leaves

Bean sprouts

Sliced cucumbers

Sliced chiles

Lime wedges

1. In a small bowl, stir together the flour, cornstarch, baking powder, turmeric, salt, and cayenne.

2. In a large bowl, whisk together the egg, vinegar, and beer. Using a silicone spatula, fold the flour mixture into the beer mixture. It should have the consistency of thin pancake batter and may be a bit lumpy. Add more beer as needed to achieve the desired consistency.

3. Preheat the oven to 250 degrees F. Pour about 2 inches oil into a large, high-sided skillet and heat over high heat to 375 degrees F. Line a rimmed baking sheet with paper towels.

4. Dip the crabs, one at a time, into the batter and allow the excess to drip off. Holding the crab by the shell flaps, carefully lower the crab legs and body into the hot oil. Wait for a few seconds and then lower the entire crab into the oil. Repeat with the other crabs, but don't crowd the pan; work in batches as necessary. Cook until golden and crispy, 6–8 minutes per side. Transfer to the paper towels to drain and keep warm in the oven until all the crabs are ready.

5. To serve, cut each crab in half. Wrap a half crab in a lettuce leaf, add some of the herbs and vegetables, fold it taco style, and dip it in nước chấm sauce (recipe follows).

★ Nước Chấm ★

½ cup freshly squeezed lime juice

½ cup water

6 tablespoons fish sauce

2 tablespoons sweet chili sauce, such as Mae Ploy

½ cup sugar

3 garlic cloves, minced

½ teaspoon red pepper flakes

1. Combine all the ingredients in a small bowl and stir until the sugar dissolves. Set aside or chill until ready to use.

Bajan Fish Cakes

LEANNA

When I was growing up, my parents always held my birthday parties at the house. They would rent tables, chairs, gigantic speakers, and balloon arrangements. One of my cousins or neighbors would DJ, and some kind of entertainment was booked for the children. The menu varied from year to year, but there were two things that would always make the list: my mom's elaborate birthday cakes (like, seriously impressive cakes) and fish cakes. These delicious salted cod fritters can be made as spicy as you like with Bajan hot pepper sauce, a Barbadian-style yellow hot sauce made from Scotch bonnet chiles. If you can't find it, you can use your favorite hot sauce. **Serves 6**

Fish cakes

8 ounces boneless salted cod fillets

½ cup minced white onion

2 garlic cloves, minced

½ cup chopped fresh parsley

Leaves from 4 thyme sprigs

1 teaspoon ground black pepper, or to taste

2 tablespoons Bajan hot pepper sauce, or to taste

2 tablespoons unsalted butter, softened

1¼ cups all-purpose flour

2 tablespoons baking powder

1 large egg, beaten

¾ cup whole milk

¼ cup water

Vegetable oil, for frying

Dipping sauce

½ cup mayonnaise

Juice of ½ lime

2 teaspoons Sriracha

1–2 teaspoons chopped fresh parsley or chives

1. In a medium pot, bring 2 quarts water to a boil over medium-high heat. Add the salted cod and boil for 5 minutes. Drain the water from the pot, leaving the fish in the pot. Add 2 quarts fresh water to the pot, bring to a boil again, and boil for another 5 minutes. Repeat this process up to 6 times. (The purpose of this process is to boil out the excess salt from the fish so that it is not too salty. Pinch a small piece of the fish after boiling to make sure you like it. If it is still too salty for your taste, just repeat until it tastes the way you like it.) Drain and transfer the fish to a medium bowl.

2. Using a fork, flake the fish. Add the onion, garlic, parsley, and thyme and mix well. Stir in the black pepper and Bajan pepper sauce and mix well. Stir in the butter and mix vigorously to make sure there are no chunks of butter. Add the flour, baking powder, egg, milk, and water. Stir until you have a chunky batter.

3. Pour about 1 inch oil into a large skillet and heat over medium heat to 350 degrees F. Using a tablespoon, carefully spoon the batter into the skillet to make each fish cake. The fish cakes should not touch while frying, so work in batches as necessary. Fry the first side of the fish cakes until golden brown, 5–6 minutes, then use a slotted spoon to carefully turn the fish cakes over and fry the other side until golden brown, another 5–6 minutes. Transfer the fish cakes to a paper towel–lined plate.

4. While the fish cakes are cooking, make the dipping sauce. Combine the mayonnaise, lime juice, sriracha, and parsley in a bowl and stir until fully incorporated.

5. Serve the fish cakes with the dipping sauce.

Saltfish and Ackee with Fried Dumplings

LEANNA

Even though my family isn't from Jamaica, I grew up eating ackee and saltfish: a dish of salt cod mixed with ackee, the national fruit of Jamaica. Our neighborhood in the Bronx was a community of Caribbean immigrants. When we had block parties, Easter brunches, and barbecues, the smorgasbord of food was epic. To this day, it is one of my favorite breakfast/brunch dishes. It's actually pretty simple to make as long as you can get your hands on the main ingredients. In this dish, I match it up with some simple fried dumplings on the side.

When cooked, it may look like scrambled eggs, but ackee is actually a fruit that grows on a tree. When it is ripe, the ackee is picked from the tree, the seeds are taken out, and the fruit is canned for sale. It typically comes in a 15-ounce can that can be found in the Caribbean or international aisle of your local grocery store. Ackee can be a little pricey, but if you ask me, it's totally worth it. **Serves 6**

Saltfish and ackee

- 1 pound boneless salted cod or pollock fillets
- 3 tablespoons vegetable oil
- 1 medium tomato, chopped
- 1 small red or white onion, chopped
- 1 scallion, thinly sliced
- 2 garlic cloves, minced
- 1 Scotch bonnet pepper, minced
- 1 teaspoon finely ground black pepper
- 1 (15-ounce) can ackee in salt water, drained

Fried dumplings

- 4 cups all-purpose flour, divided
- 2 tablespoons packed light brown sugar
- 1 tablespoon baking powder
- 1 teaspoon iodized salt
- ⅓ cup water
- 1½ tablespoons unsalted butter, melted
- ½ cup whole milk
- Vegetable oil, for frying

1. In a medium pot, bring 3 quarts water to a boil over medium-high heat. Add the salted fish and boil for 5 minutes. Drain the water, leaving the fish in the pot. Add 3 quarts fresh water, bring to a boil again, and boil for another 5 minutes. Repeat this process up to 6 times. (The purpose of this process is to boil out the excess salt from the fish. Pinch a small piece of the fish after boiling to make sure you like it. If it is still too salty, just repeat until it tastes the way you like it.) Drain and transfer the fish to a medium bowl. Using a fork, flake the fish into small pieces.

2. While the fish is boiling, start the dumplings. In a large bowl, combine 3 cups of the flour, the brown sugar, baking powder, salt, water, and melted butter. Using your hands, mix until everything is fully incorporated. Add the the milk and remaining 1 cup flour and mix, using your hands, until fully incorporated. Cover the bowl and refrigerate for 30 minutes.

3. Divide the dough into 12 equal balls, slightly larger than a golf ball.

4. In a large, heavy-bottomed skillet, heat about ½ inch oil over medium heat to 350–375 degrees F. Working in batches as necessary, fry the dumplings, turning often, until golden brown all over, 4–5 minutes. Transfer to a paper towel–lined plate.

5. Heat the oil in a large skillet over medium heat. Add the tomato, onion, scallion, garlic, and Scotch bonnet pepper and sauté for 2–3 minutes. Stir in the flaked fish and black pepper and sauté for another 2–3 minutes. Add the ackee and sauté for 4 minutes. Serve warm with the dumplings.

S'feeha and Manakish

Meat and Za'atar Cheese Pies

SALMAH

S'feeha and manakish—bread dough filled with lamb or za'atar-cheese filling—hold a special place in my heart, as the recipes were taught to me by a dear friend who opened my eyes to a whole new world of spices. These simple brunch pies drew me into the indulgence of a Lebanese breakfast spread, with conversations unspooling over warm meat and cheese pies, accompanied by olives, cucumbers, and a cool yogurt mint sauce (see the sauce recipe with my Chicken Chapli Kebabs, page 99). **Makes 10 pies**

1. In a large bowl, whisk together the flour, yeast, sugar, and salt. Add the milk and oil and mix with a wooden spoon to form a dough. Knead with your hands for about 8 minutes to make a smooth, round ball. Place the dough ball in a lightly oiled bowl. Cover with a clean, damp kitchen towel and set aside to rise for 40 minutes.

2. Meanwhile, to make the lamb filling, in a food processor, process the ground lamb, onion, tomato, parsley, garlic, jalapeño, allspice, and pomegranate molasses until smooth. To make the cheese filling, combine the cheeses, oil, and za'atar in a bowl.

3. Preheat the oven to 350 degrees F. Line two rimmed baking sheets with parchment.

4. Divide the dough into 10 small balls and roll into thin disks about ¼ to ½ inch thick.

5. Divide the lamb mixture among half of the dough disks, spreading it to about ½ inch of the edges. Place the meat pies on one baking sheet.

6. Divide the cheese mixture among the remaining dough disks. Fold the sides of the dough up and over to create a boat shape, then pinch the top and bottom edges together. Place the cheese pies on another baking sheet.

7. Bake for 15 minutes, or until the dough is golden brown and the fillings are cooked through. Serve warm, garnished with pine nuts and scallions if desired.

Dough

3 cups all-purpose flour

1 packet fast-acting instant yeast

2 teaspoons sugar

Pinch salt

1½ cups milk

⅓ cup vegetable oil

Lamb filling

1 pound ground lamb

1 medium onion, roughly chopped

1 large tomato, roughly chopped

½ cup chopped fresh parsley

5 garlic cloves, peeled

1 jalapeño pepper

½ teaspoon ground allspice

2 tablespoons plus 1 teaspoon pomegranate molasses

Sliced scallions, for garnish, optional

Pine nuts, for garnish, optional

Cheese and za'atar filling

1 cup shredded halloumi cheese

½ cup shredded mozzarella cheese

¼ cup olive oil

¼ cup za'atar

Pine nuts, for garnish, optional

Spam Katsu Musubi and Mochiko Chicken Musubi

RELLE

Musubi is a version of Japanese onigiri (stuffed rice balls). While not a traditional Hawaiian dish, musubi is definitely a local favorite—especially Spam musubi, which are ubiquitous. Marinated Spam is breaded and fried to golden-brown perfection, then sandwiched between a bed of sticky white rice and wrapped in nori. Another staple is mochiko chicken musubi, made from fried chicken that's been sprinkled with mochiko flour (glutinous rice flour, sometimes called sweet rice flour) for an extra crispy exterior. Together, these musubi make the ultimate snack or on-the-go meal. **Makes 8 musubi**

Rice

4 cups medium-grain white rice, such as Hinode

4 cups water

Mochiko chicken musubi

¼ cup potato starch

¼ cup mochiko flour

¼ cup sugar

¼ cup thinly sliced scallions

1 tablespoon sesame seeds

1 teaspoon minced garlic

1 teaspoon minced ginger

½ teaspoon salt

¼ cup soy sauce

2 large eggs, beaten

1 pound boneless, skinless chicken thighs, cut into strips

Vegetable oil, for frying

4 sheets nori, cut in half

8 teaspoons furikake, divided

Spam musubi

3 tablespoons soy sauce

3 tablespoons sugar

1 (12-ounce) can low-sodium Spam, sliced lengthwise into 8 slices

½ cup all-purpose flour

2 large eggs

½ cup panko bread crumbs

Vegetable oil, for frying

4 sheets nori, cut in half

8 teaspoons furikake, divided

1. First, make the rice. Rinse the rice under cool running water until the water runs clear, then drain. Put the rice and water in a rice cooker and set to cook. While the rice is cooking, prepare the fillings.

2. To make the mochiko chicken filling, in a large bowl, combine the potato starch, mochiko flour, sugar, scallions, sesame seeds, garlic, ginger, salt, soy sauce, and eggs. Whisk to combine. Add the chicken and stir to combine. Transfer to a resealable plastic bag and place in the refrigerator to marinate for 10 minutes.

3. In a large skillet, heat ½ inch oil over medium heat to 325 degrees F. Set a wire rack over a rimmed baking sheet.

4. Remove the chicken from the marinade and carefully place it in the oil. Fry until golden brown on both sides and cooked through, 10–15 minutes. Transfer the chicken to the rack. Retain the oil (remove from heat while you prepare the spam katsu).

(recipe continues)

5. To make the spam katsu, in a large bowl, whisk together the soy sauce and sugar until well combined. Put the sliced Spam in the sauce mixture and turn to coat both sides. Allow to marinate at room temperature for 15 minutes.

6. While the Spam is marinating, set up the breading station. In a shallow dish, put the flour. In another shallow dish, whisk the eggs. In a third shallow dish, put the panko.

7. Remove the Spam from the marinade. Coat one slice of Spam first in flour, then in egg, and finally in panko. Set aside and repeat with the remainder of the Spam. Return the skillet with the oil to the heat (add more oil if needed). Working in batches, add the breaded Spam to the oil and fry until golden brown on the first side, 2–3 minutes. Flip and repeat on the other side. Transfer to the rack with the chicken to drain.

8. To form the Spam musubi, lay a piece of nori on a work surface. Place a musubi mold (or Spam can with the bottom removed) in the center of the nori. Press ¼ cup rice into the musubi mold. Sprinkle ½ teaspoon furikake over the rice. Layer on a slice of Spam. Sprinkle with another ½ teaspoon furikake. Top with another ¼ cup rice. Press the musubi out of the mold. Wrap the nori around the musubi and seal the ends with a small dab of water. Continue with the remainder of the Spam.

9. To form the mochiko chicken musubi, lay a piece of nori on a work surface. Place a musubi mold in the center of the nori. Press ¼ cup rice into the mold and sprinkle with ½ teaspoon furikake. Top with a piece of chicken and press the musubi out of the mold. Wrap the nori around the musubi and seal the ends with a small dab of water. Continue with the remainder of the chicken.

Soups and Stews

(and Things to Go with Them)

Bison Pho 37

Caribbean Delight 38
(Stewed Oxtails with Rice and Gandules)

Elk Stew 40

Gandule Rice and Pastele Stew 42

T'becha with Couscous 44
(Short Rib, String Bean, and Potato Stew)

Hominy Red Chile Stew 46

Lasagna Soup with Garlic Knots 47

**Portuguese Bean Soup
with Cornbread** 50

Sancocho 52
(Meat and Vegetable Stew)

Meaty Beef & Bean Chili 53

Pepperpot 55
(Cassareep-Braised Beef Stew)

Matzah Ball Soup 56

Three Sisters Soup with Fry Bread 58

Salmorejo 61
(Spanish Chilled Tomato Soup)

Bison Pho

Members of the Coeur d'Alene tribe travel across the Rocky Mountains from northern Idaho to hunt buffalo in Montana. On these travels, young ones leave as children and come home as adults. When I think about the time of my life when I arrived as a child but left as an adult, I think of my years at the University of Washington in Seattle. Seattle is home to hundreds of mom-and-pop pho shops. This is where I fell in love with pho. I incorporated my favorite, bison steak, into this Seattle staple to represent my own journey into adulthood. **Serves 6**

MARIA

1. Position an oven rack in the highest position and preheat the broiler. Line a rimmed baking sheet with aluminum foil.

2. Put the onions and ginger on the prepared baking sheet and broil for 10–15 minutes, turning the onions and ginger occasionally so that they become charred on all sides.

3. Meanwhile, put the cinnamon sticks, coriander seeds, fennel seeds, star anise, cloves, and black cardamom pod in a small skillet. Toast the spices over low heat, stirring occasionally, until fragrant, about 5 minutes. Transfer the toasted spices to a cotton muslin bag/herb sachet.

4. In a stockpot, bring the bone broth to a boil over high heat, then lower to a gentle simmer. Add the charred onions and ginger and the bag of toasted spices. Add the salt, fish sauce, and rock sugar. Simmer the broth for 45 minutes, then strain through a fine-mesh strainer and keep warm.

5. While the broth is simmering, prepare the rice vermicelli according to the package directions. Drain and set aside.

6. Heat the oil in a large skillet over high heat. Add the bison steaks and lightly sear, 4–5 minutes on each side. Allow to rest for 2 minutes, then slice thinly against the grain.

7. To serve, divide the noodles evenly among 6 bowls. Top with the sliced bison steak. Ladle in enough stock to cover the noodles and steak. Serve with the cilantro, Thai basil, jalapeño, bean sprouts, and lime wedges.

2 yellow onions, peeled and quartered

4-inch piece ginger, halved lengthwise

2 cinnamon sticks

1 tablespoon coriander seeds

1 tablespoon fennel seeds

6 star anise

6 whole cloves

1 black cardamom pod

2 quarts bison bone broth

1½ tablespoons salt

¼ cup fish sauce

1-inch piece yellow rock sugar

1 (14-ounce) package Vietnamese rice vermicelli

1–2 tablespoons vegetable oil

2 (8-ounce) boneless bison steaks

1 bunch cilantro

1 bunch Thai basil

1 jalapeño, thinly sliced

2 cups bean sprouts

Lime wedges, for serving

Caribbean Delight

Stewed Oxtails with Rice and Gandules (Peas)

Before you even get started on this recipe, I need you to know, this is a two-day process. The oxtails must be marinated overnight and then cooked for 3–4 hours. In other words, don't you come home from a long day of work thinking that you can just whip up some oxtails. It takes a while, but I promise, it is well worth the wait. Serve with my Fried Plantains (page 13) for the full experience.

Oxtails are without question my husband's favorite dish. When done right, the meat falls off the bones like shredded beef. The gravy is thick and rich and a little bit spicy. My husband will routinely save the sauce, even after all of the oxtails have been eaten, to pour over a bowl of rice or eat with a nice chunk of fresh bread. It is not uncommon to find him in the kitchen, standing over the pot, bread in hand, ready to dip it into the gravy. **Serves 6**

1. In a large bowl, combine the paprika, black pepper, salt, oxtail seasoning, onion, garlic, scallions, 4 of the thyme sprigs, and the hot sauce. Add the oxtails and toss them with the spices until evenly coated. Cover the bowl and allow the oxtails to marinate in the refrigerator overnight.

2. The next day, empty the oxtails into a large pot. Pour in 3 cups of the beef broth and bring to a boil over medium-high heat, stirring occasionally. Boil for 15 minutes, then turn the heat down to a low simmer and cover the pot. Cook the oxtails for 2 hours, stirring occasionally. Add a little of the remaining 1 cup beef broth if the liquid level gets low.

3. Add the browning sauce and remaining 2 thyme sprigs, cover, and allow the oxtails to cook for another hour, stirring occasionally. Be sure to watch the liquid levels and add more broth as needed.

4. Add the butter beans and red pepper flakes and stir. Cover and cook for 30 more minutes, stirring occasionally. While the oxtails are cooking, make the rice and peas.

5. Combine the garlic, scallions, thyme, pigeon peas, coconut milk, and salt in a Dutch oven and bring to a boil over medium-high heat, stirring frequently. Turn it down to a simmer, add the rice, and give everything a good stir. Cover and cook, stirring occasionally, until the liquid has evaporated and the rice grains are separated and fluffy, about 20 minutes. Season with salt.

6. Serve the oxtails with the rice and peas.

Stewed oxtails

3 tablespoons paprika

2 tablespoons black pepper

2 tablespoons iodized salt

2 tablespoons oxtail seasoning

1 large yellow onion, diced

6 garlic cloves, minced

2 scallions, chopped

6 thyme sprigs, divided

¼ cup Louisiana Hot Sauce

5 pounds oxtails

3–4 cups beef broth, divided

2 tablespoons Caribbean browning sauce

2 (15-ounce) cans butter beans, drained and rinsed

2 teaspoons red pepper flakes

Rice and peas

4–5 garlic cloves, peeled and smashed

2 scallions, roots trimmed and stalks bruised with a knife

4–6 thyme sprigs

2 (15.5-ounce) cans pigeon peas, drained and rinsed

2 (13.5-ounce) cans coconut milk

Iodized salt to taste

3–4 cups jasmine or basmati rice, rinsed in cold water and drained

Elk Stew

Elk stew is a Coeur d'Alene staple. We have elk stew at almost every ceremony, feast, and gathering. Make sure to soak your elk in milk before you cook with it to reduce any gaminess in the meat. Even a few minutes will do the trick! Keep it simple or serve with a piece of Fry Bread (page 59) and you have a perfect winter meal. **Serves 10**

½ cup all-purpose flour

Salt and ground black pepper to taste

1 pound elk stew meat

2 tablespoons olive oil, divided

1 onion, diced

2 large carrots, diced

4 celery stalks, diced

1 turnip or rutabaga, peeled and diced

4 garlic cloves, peeled and lightly smashed

1 quart beef stock

Fresh herb sprigs, such as thyme and rosemary

2 Idaho potatoes, peeled and diced

1. In a medium bowl, season the flour with salt and pepper. Dredge the elk meat in the seasoned flour.

2. In a Dutch oven, heat 1 tablespoon of the olive oil over medium-high heat. Add the elk meat and sear until browned on all sides, 2–3 minutes. Transfer to a plate.

3. Add the remaining 1 tablespoon oil to the same pot and heat over medium-high heat. Add the onion, carrots, celery, turnip, and garlic and cook, stirring, until slightly soft, 5–7 minutes. Deglaze the pan with the beef stock. Return the meat to the pot, along with the herbs. Reduce the heat to low and cook, covered, until the meat is tender enough to cut with a fork, 45 minutes total.

4. About 20 minutes before the end of cooking time, add the potatoes to the pot and let simmer with the other ingredients until tender. Serve hot.

Gandule Rice and Pastele Stew

RELLE

This tender pork stew, served with a dish of gandules (pigeon peas) and coconut rice, is one of my husband's favorite meals. Both components show the influence of Puerto Rico on Hawaiian cuisine. In the early 1900s, two hurricanes hit Puerto Rico and devastated the sugar plantations there, leading to a shortage . . . and building a huge demand for Hawaiian sugar. Puerto Rican laborers moved to Hawai'i and brought delicious recipes with them, notably pasteles and arroz con gandule, or as we call it, gandule rice. Pasteles are traditional Latin American/Caribbean foods similar to tamales. Classic pasteles are made using a banana leaf as a wrap, stuffed with masa made of green banana paste and a meat mixture, tied up, and cooked. Quite the labor of love to make!

If you love pasteles, you'll love this recipe for pastele stew, which is like that dish deconstructed—tender pork chunks infused with classic Puerto Rican flavors of garlic, onion, cilantro, and achiote. Perfect for anytime, but especially in the cooler months. **Serves 10**

Pastele stew

3 tablespoons achiote oil

3 pounds pork butt, cubed

4 garlic cloves, chopped

1 onion, diced

Hawaiian salt and ground black pepper to taste

1 (6-ounce) can tomato paste

6 cups water

3 bunches Chinese parsley, roughly chopped

1 (6-ounce) can large whole pitted black olives, drained

Gandule rice

1 tablespoon achiote oil

8 ounces bacon, cut into ½-inch pieces

8 ounces pork tenderloin, sliced into short, narrow strips

4 garlic cloves, finely minced

½ green bell pepper, diced

1 small onion, diced

1 bunch cilantro, finely chopped

5 scallions, thinly sliced

3 cups white rice

3 cups chicken broth

2 packets Sazón Goya

1 (8-ounce) can tomato sauce

1 (15-ounce) can gandules verdes, drained and rinsed

1 (6-ounce) can pitted black olives, drained

Plantain dumplings

2 large green plantains, peeled

¼ teaspoon Sazón Goya

---

1. To make the pastele stew, heat the achiote oil in a large pot over medium-high heat. Add the pork, garlic, onion, salt, and pepper and sauté the pork until browned, 3–5 minutes. Add the tomato paste, water, and parsley and stir to combine.

2. Lower the heat to medium-low and simmer, covered, until the meat is tender, about 1 hour. If you like your meat more tender, you can cook for a longer amount of time. Once the meat reaches the desired tenderness, add the olives and stir to heat through.

3. While the meat is simmering, make the gandule rice. Heat the achiote oil in a large skillet over medium-high heat. Add the bacon and pork and sauté until browned, 5–10 minutes. Add the garlic, bell pepper, and onion and cook until fragrant and the onion becomes translucent, 2–3 minutes. Add the cilantro and scallions and stir to combine and heat through. Remove the skillet from the heat and set aside.

4. Rinse the rice under cool running water until the water runs clear, then drain. Put the rice in a rice cooker. Add the chicken broth, Sazón Goya, tomato sauce, gandule beans, and olives.

5. Pour off the oil from the bacon mixture and discard. Add the bacon mixture to the rice cooker and stir until well combined. Set the rice cooker to cook. Once the rice cooker has finished, open and fluff the rice with a fork.

6. When the stew is nearly done, make the plantain dumplings. Put the plantains in a food processor and blend until smooth. Add the Sazón Goya and blend until just combined. Scoop about 1 tablespoon of the mixture and add it to the pot of pastele stew. Repeat with the remaining mixture, being careful not to place the dough balls on top of one another. Cook until heated through, 3–5 minutes.

7. Serve the pastele stew and plantain dumplings alongside the gandule rice.

T'becha with Couscous

Short Rib, String Bean, and Potato Stew with Couscous

BRAD

I have been eating this magical Libyan short rib stew since I was six months old, and it is a weekly Shabbat dinner staple in my household. The week does not feel complete without t'becha simmering away on the stove on Friday. This dish is packed with flavor—spicy, savory, and all-around delicious. The short ribs are tender and melt in your mouth, making this a dish I dream about. **Serves 6**

4 pounds bone-in beef ribs, cut flanken style (see note) into 1½-inch-thick strips, at room temperature

1½ tablespoons kosher salt, plus more for sprinkling

Ground black pepper to taste

2 tablespoons vegetable oil

1 onion, chopped

1 (6-ounce) can tomato paste

1½ tablespoons baharat spice

1 tablespoon hot paprika

1 tablespoon sweet paprika

1 teaspoon ground cinnamon

2 teaspoons chicken consommé powder

8 beef marrow bones, cut into 1- to 1½-inch rounds

4 sweet potatoes, peeled and cut in halves or thirds

4 Yukon Gold potatoes, peeled and cut in half

1 pound frozen green peas

8 ounces string beans

1 batch cooked couscous (page 152), for serving

Note: Flanken cut short ribs are cut across the bones so each slice of meat contains a few pieces of bone, resulting in more delicate meat.

1. Pat the beef dry and sprinkle salt and pepper on all sides.

2. Working in batches as needed, heat the oil in a Dutch oven over medium-high heat. Add the meat and brown well on all sides, 3–4 minutes per side. Transfer the beef to a plate.

3. Add the onion to the pot and sauté until translucent, about 5 minutes.

4. Return the beef to the pot and pour in just enough water to cover. Bring to a boil and boil for 40 minutes.

5. While the meat is boiling, prepare the sauce mixture. In a large bowl combine the tomato paste, baharat, both paprikas, the salt, pepper to taste, cinnamon, and consommé powder. Add just enough water to create a watery paste (about 1 cup). Add the sauce to the pot and cook for 10 minutes.

6. Add the marrow bones, sweet potatoes, Yukon Gold potatoes, and frozen peas, bring to a boil, and simmer for 1 hour.

7. Add the string beans to the top of the stew, sprinkle with a little salt and pepper, and simmer until the meat pulls away from the bone, another 1–1½ hours. Serve with couscous.

Hominy Red Chile Stew

MARIA

After a long weekend away, I came home to an empty house with only a few things in my cabinet and freezer: a pork shoulder, onion, red chile sauce, and a can of hominy. I threw it all together with no intention of creating anything special. When I tasted it, I was so excited that a little experiment, created out of necessity, could yield such delicious results. This is now in my rotation for weeknight comfort food. **Serves 8**

Red chile sauce

8 ounces California or New Mexico red chiles, stems, seeds, and ribs removed

6 tablespoons all-purpose flour, divided

4 garlic cloves, peeled, divided

1 tablespoon salt, divided

Stew

Vegetable oil, for cooking

1 (4–6-pound) pork shoulder

1 onion, diced

2 red bell peppers, seeded and diced

1 (15-ounce) can hominy, drained

1 (14.5-ounce) can diced tomatoes

Cooked white rice, for serving

1 bunch cilantro, for garnish

1. To make the red chile sauce, put the chiles in a large pot and add enough water to just cover them. Bring the water to a boil over high heat, then lower the heat, cover, and simmer for 20 minutes, turning the chiles over with tongs halfway through to make sure they soften evenly. Drain the chiles and let them cool slightly.

2. Put half of the chiles in a blender along with 3 cups fresh water, 3 tablespoons of the flour, 2 of the garlic cloves, and ½ tablespoon of the salt. Blend the mixture until smooth. Strain the sauce through a fine-mesh strainer to remove any skins and seeds. Repeat the blending and straining process with the remaining chiles, another 3 cups fresh water, and the remaining flour, garlic, and salt. If necessary, season with more salt. Chill if made in advance, or use in the stew immediately.

3. To make the stew, set an Instant Pot to medium-high heat in sauté mode. Coat the bottom of the pot with vegetable oil and add the pork shoulder. Sear all sides until nicely browned, 4–5 minutes on each side. Close the lid and set to sealing. Cook on high pressure for 40 minutes. Release the steam naturally and let the meat cool down slightly.

4. Coat the bottom of a Dutch oven with vegetable oil and heat over medium-high heat. Add the onion and red bell peppers and sauté until the onion is translucent, about 5 minutes. Add the hominy, tomatoes with their juices, and red chile sauce. Let the mixture come to a boil, then reduce the heat to a low simmer.

5. When the pork shoulder is cooled enough to touch, tear it into small pieces and add the meat to the red sauce. Let simmer until heated through and the flavors have melded.

6. To serve, scoop some rice into each serving bowl. Ladle the pork mixture over the rice and garnish with fresh cilantro.

Lasagna Soup with Garlic Knots

LEANNA

If you have ever made lasagna from scratch, you know that the payoff is always worth it, but it is a lot of work and it takes time. So what do you do when you are in the mood for lasagna, but you have neither the time nor the energy that it requires? You make my lasagna soup, of course, and satisfy that craving in a fraction of the time. And, when you do have the time to kick things up a notch, you can whip up some garlic knots to go with it. Because who doesn't love a side of bread with soup?

For me, this recipe brings back all the feels of heading to the local Italian restaurant with my grandpa. Sure, it's not a traditional lasagna like we enjoyed there together, but it has all the flavors that make it feel like one. I like to think that if he were still alive, he would love this recipe hack. Because although my grandpa wasn't really much of a cook, he sure did love to eat. **Serves 6**

(recipe continues)

1 teaspoon extra virgin
olive oil

1 pound ground beef

8 ounces ground Italian
sausage

5 garlic cloves, chopped

1 small white onion,
chopped

1 tablespoon dried basil

1 tablespoon dried oregano

1 teaspoon dried marjoram

2 (14.5-ounce) cans Italian-
style diced tomatoes

3 tablespoons tomato paste

1 quart beef broth

8 lasagna noodles, broken
into small pieces

8 ounces ricotta cheese

4 ounces Parmesan cheese,
grated, plus more for
serving

4 ounces mozzarella cheese,
shredded

Salt and ground black
pepper to taste

Chopped fresh parsley,
for garnish

1. Set the Instant Pot to sauté and heat the olive oil. Add the beef and sausage and cook, stirring often, until browned, 8–10 minutes. Add the garlic and onion and cook until the onion is translucent, 3–4 minutes. Add the basil, oregano, marjoram, tomatoes with their juices, tomato paste, beef broth, and noodles and stir well. Press "cancel," close the lid, and set to sealing. Cook at high pressure for 20 minutes, then press "cancel" and release the pressure.

2. In a medium bowl, combine the ricotta, Parmesan, and mozzarella and stir until blended.

3. Open the Instant Pot and stir the soup. Give it a taste and season with salt and pepper as desired. Ladle the soup into serving bowls, top with a dollop of the ricotta mixture, and sprinkle with parsley and more Parmesan if desired.

★ Garlic Knots ★

2 teaspoons instant yeast
½ teaspoon sugar
1 cup warm water (105–110°F)
2½ cups all-purpose flour
1 teaspoon iodized salt
8 tablespoons (1 stick) unsalted butter, melted
4–6 garlic cloves, minced
1 bunch parsley, roughly chopped
Grated Parmesan cheese, for sprinkling

1. Put the yeast, sugar, and warm water in the bowl of an electric mixer and give it a quick whisk. Set the bowl aside and allow the yeast to bloom, 1–2 minutes.

2. Add the flour and the salt. Using the dough hook, knead the dough for 5 minutes at medium-low speed. If the dough does not form a ball or pull away from the sides of the bowl, add more flour, 1 tablespoon at a time, until a ball is formed.

3. Lift the dough out of the bowl briefly to oil the mixing bowl with olive oil, then return the dough to the bowl. Cover the bowl with a clean, damp towel and set aside to allow the dough to rise to about 1½ times its original size, 50–60 minutes.

4. Preheat the oven to 400 degrees F. Lightly grease a rimmed baking sheet.

5. Place the dough on a lightly floured work surface. Cut the dough into 16 pieces of equal size and roll each piece into a long rope. Form each rope into a knot by making an upside-down U, crossing the "legs," pulling one leg through the opening, and then tucking both underneath. Place the knots on the prepared baking sheet.

6. In a small bowl, stir together the melted butter, garlic, and parsley. Brush each knot with the garlic butter. Bake for 20 minutes. When done baking and still warm, brush with any excess garlic butter and sprinkle with Parmesan.

Portuguese Bean Soup with Cornbread and Liliko'i Butter

RELLE

If you grew up in Hawai'i, you've probably had Portuguese bean soup! It seems like every family has its own take on this dish. Portuguese food is a large part of Hawaiian-style cuisine because of the Portuguese immigrants who came to Hawai'i in the late 1800s and early 1900s to work on plantations. Portuguese bean soup is Hawai'i comfort food at its finest: hearty tomato-based soup brimming with smoked ham hock, Portuguese sausage, kidney beans, and veggies. Served alongside a moist cornbread muffin with tangy liliko'i (passion fruit) butter, this is the perfect soup to feed your family. **Serves 10**

6 cups water

4 (8-ounce) cans tomato sauce

3 smoked ham hocks

1 (5-ounce) mild Portuguese sausage, sliced into coins

4 ounces center-sliced smoked ham

1 (15.5-ounce) can dark red kidney beans, drained and rinsed

1 cup diced celery

2 small potatoes, diced

3 carrots, peeled and diced

½ onion, diced

1 cup macaroni

1 cup chopped watercress

1. Set an Instant Pot to sauté. Add the water and tomato sauce and stir to combine. Add the ham hocks, Portuguese sausage, ham, and kidney beans. Close the lid and set to sealing. Cook on high pressure for 35 minutes.

2. Once the cooking is complete, turn the knob to venting and allow a quick release. If the soup begins to sputter out of the vent control, release by slowly letting out pressure for a second or two at a time. Once the pressure has released, add the celery, potatoes, carrots, onion, and macaroni. Seal again and cook on high pressure for 3 minutes, then allow a quick release, again using a controlled release if needed.

3. Remove the lid and stir in the watercress. Serve the soup with cornbread muffins and liliko'i butter (recipes follow).

★ Cornbread ★

2 cups Bisquick

½ cup sugar

1½ tablespoons cornmeal

½ teaspoon baking powder

1 cup whole milk

2 large eggs

12 tablespoons (1½ sticks) unsalted butter, melted and cooled

1. Preheat the oven to 350 degrees F. Spray a 12-cup muffin tin with nonstick cooking spray and line with paper liners.

2. In a large bowl, whisk together the Bisquick, sugar, cornmeal, and baking powder until well combined.

3. In a medium bowl, whisk together the milk, eggs, and melted butter until well combined. Add the wet ingredients to the dry ingredients and stir until just combined. Pour the batter into the prepared muffin cups to fill about three-quarters of the way.

4. Bake for 25–30 minutes, until golden brown. Set aside to cool.

★ Liliko'i Butter ★

4 large eggs

1 cup sugar

½ cup liliko'i juice (passion fruit juice)

6 tablespoons unsalted butter, cubed

1. Pour an inch or so of water into a medium saucepan and bring to a simmer over medium heat. Set a small heatproof bowl over the boiling water; make sure the bottom of the bowl doesn't touch the water.

2. Put the eggs and sugar in the bowl and whisk well to combine. Add the liliko'i juice and whisk to incorporate. Once well combined, add the butter. Stir with a silicone spatula until the liquid begins to thicken and is able to coat the back of a spoon, 10–15 minutes.

3. Remove the bowl and let it cool, then place it in the refrigerator to set.

Sancocho

Meat and Vegetable Stew

LEANNA

I traveled to Punta Cana on a food tour in search of some of the best food that the Dominican Republic has to offer. While I was there, I enjoyed a delicious traditional Latin American dish called sancocho, a soup made with meat (traditionally, beef), pumpkin, and vegetables. According to one of the waiters at the resort restaurant, it is the ultimate hangover cure. I'm not too sure about that part, but what I am sure of is that sancocho is downright delicious. **Serves 8**

1 pound beef stew meat, cubed

1 lime, cut in half

2 garlic cloves, minced

¼ cup chopped fresh parsley

1½ pounds chicken drumettes

1 tablespoon adobo seasoning

1 teaspoon dried oregano

1 teaspoon paprika

2 tablespoons salt, plus more if needed

2 tablespoons vegetable oil

6 cups water

1 cup chicken broth

1 smoked ham hock

2 white yams, peeled and cut into 1-inch cubes

1 white sweet potato, peeled and cut into 1-inch cubes

1 chayote, peeled and cut into 1-inch cubes

½ small pumpkin, peeled, halved, seeded, and cut into 1-inch cubes

2 firm, yellow plantains, peeled and cut into 2-inch sections

15 pequiin chiles

1. Put the beef in a medium bowl. Squeeze the juice of one lime half over the beef. Add the garlic and parsley and stir. Cover the bowl and refrigerate for at least 30 minutes.

2. Put the chicken in another medium bowl and squeeze the remaining lime half over the chicken. Sprinkle the adobo, oregano, paprika, and salt over the chicken, stir, and set aside.

3. Heat the oil in a large cast iron pot over medium-high heat. Add the beef and brown for 2–3 minutes, then lower to medium heat, cover the pot, and cook for 15 minutes. Add a few tablespoons of water if necessary to make sure that the beef does not burn.

4. Add the chicken drumettes and stir, then cover the pot again and cook for 5 minutes.

5. Add the water, chicken broth, and ham hock and bring to a boil. Turn the heat down to medium and add the yams, sweet potato, and chayote. Stir the soup, cover partially, and cook for 15 minutes, stirring occasionally.

6. Add the pumpkin and plantains to the soup. Stir, cover partially, and cook for 10 minutes.

7. Add the chiles and cook for 3 more minutes. Remove the ham hock. Taste and add more salt if needed. Serve.

Meaty Beef & Bean Chili

Everyone in my family makes chili, and everyone makes it differently. It's like we're Goldilocks and the Three Bears. My sister's is mild and uses red beans. My mom likes hers a little spicy with more veggies. My brother would use kidney beans and jalapeños. I like to use different meats and black beans and—my secret—blend in a can of chipotles in adobo. They give it a smoky-sweet heat that is just fantastic. Plus, I love to hit the top with a variety of garnishes. Chili is also special because it makes me think of my dad. It was on the menu many Sundays when he was at my house with a crowd to watch football. We've lost my dad and my brother Kyle, and I miss them both terribly. **Serves 6**

KHELA

1. In a large Dutch oven, heat the oil over medium-high heat. Add the ground chuck, chorizo, and onions and cook, stirring often, until the ground meat is browned and broken up, 8–10 minutes. Drain most of the fat from the pan.

2. Add the tomato paste, blended chipotles, tomatoes with their juices, green chiles, garlic, cumin, and oregano to the Dutch oven. Stir to combine, then cover, reduce the heat, and simmer for 30 minutes.

3. Add the beans and ground corn chips and cook, covered, for 10 minutes.

4. Serve the chili with an assortment of garnishes.

Chili

2–3 tablespoons vegetable oil

1½ pounds ground chuck (80% lean)

12 ounces chorizo, removed from casings

2 medium onions, chopped

1 tablespoon tomato paste

1 (7-ounce) can chipotles in adobo, blended

1 (28-ounce) can petite diced tomatoes

2 (4-ounce) cans chopped green chiles

3 garlic cloves, grated

2 teaspoons ground cumin

2 teaspoons dried Mexican oregano

2 (15-ounce) cans black beans, drained and rinsed

¼ cup Fritos corn chips, ground

Garnish

Shredded sharp cheddar cheese

Chopped onions

Avocado slices

Sliced jalapeños

Sour cream

Fritos

Pepperpot

Cassareep-Braised Beef Stew

SALMAH

Pepperpot is Guyana's national dish, introduced by the Indigenous Amerindians of Guyana. This cassareep-braised beef stew is made from the tough cuts of beef. Cassareep is a thick syrup made from the extract of cassava, which is a natural preserver; a huge pot is made and can be left on the stovetop to be brought to a boil daily. The infamous sticky fingers you get from eating pepperpot come from the gelatin released after slowly braising and stewing cow heel mixed with different cuts of beef. Pepperpot is synonymous with holiday time, often enjoyed as an end-of-year feast. Of course, no pepperpot is complete without some Guyanese Plait Bread (page 237) to soak up all that goodness. **Serves 10**

1. Put the cow heel in a bowl, add the vinegar, and soak for 5 minutes. Drain, rinse the cow heel, and drain again.

2. Put the cow heel in a large pot and sauté over medium-high heat for 8 minutes, then pour in enough boiling water to cover and boil until softened, about 20 minutes. Drain.

3. Set an Instant Pot to sauté mode and add 2 teaspoons of the oil. Add the onion, garlic, and wiri wiri peppers and sauté for 5–6 minutes. Add the cow heel and sauté for 20 minutes. Close the lid and set to sealing. Cook at high pressure for 10 minutes, then release the pressure manually, press "cancel," and remove the lid.

4. Meanwhile, season the beef all over with the dried thyme, ¼ cup of the cassareep, and salt and pepper. Heat the remaining 2 teaspoons oil in a large skillet, add the beef, and cook for about 8 minutes.

5. After the Instant Pot pressure releases, add the beef, the remaining 1¾ cups cassareep, cinnamon, cloves, star anise, fresh thyme, browning sauce, and brown sugar. Seal again and cook at high pressure for 45 minutes. When finished, allow for natural release for 10 minutes, then release the steam. Serve.

---

1 pound cow heel, cut into 1½-inch sections

½ cup vinegar

2 cups boiling water

4 teaspoons vegetable oil, divided

1 large onion, diced

5 garlic cloves, minced

7 wiri wiri peppers

1½ pounds mixed beef leg and stew pieces

¼ cup dried thyme

2 cups cassareep, divided

Salt and ground black pepper to taste

5 cinnamon sticks

6 whole cloves

6 star anise

1 bundle fresh thyme

½ cup Caribbean browning sauce

¼ cup packed brown sugar

Matzah Ball Soup

BRAD

Probably the best-known Jewish food, this soup is home in a dish. Often referred to as "Jewish penicillin," matzah ball soup is the pick-me-up needed when you're under the weather or during a cold winter's night. My mom would often make matzah ball soup as an appetizer for Shabbat dinners and during the holidays, especially Passover, where matzah is the star. I swear by the boxed matzah ball mix but do add schmaltz (rendered chicken fat, which is available at butcher shops and some well-stocked grocery stores), fresh herbs, and seltzer to get them just perfectly flavored and textured.

Serves 6

Chicken broth

1 (3- to 4-pound) whole chicken

2 large onions, unpeeled and quartered

6 carrots, unpeeled and cut in thirds

3 celery stalks with leaves, cut in thirds

1 parsnip, unpeeled and cut in thirds

1 head garlic, unpeeled and cut in half crosswise

20 dill sprigs

20 parsley sprigs

15 thyme sprigs

2 tablespoons kosher salt

2 teaspoons whole black peppercorns

1½ teaspoons ground turmeric

1 teaspoon good-quality saffron

Matzah balls

2 bags (1 box) Streit's Matzo Ball Mix

2 large eggs

2 tablespoons vegetable oil

2 tablespoons schmaltz

¼ cup chopped fresh dill

¼ cup chopped fresh parsley

1 tablespoon chicken consommé powder

¼ cup seltzer

Salt, for boiling water

To serve

2 carrots, sliced into ¼-inch coins

Chopped fresh dill

---

1. Put all the chicken broth ingredients in an 8-quart Instant Pot. Add water to the max fill line. Close the lid and set to sealing. Cook at high pressure for 25 minutes. Release the pressure manually, press "cancel," and remove the lid. Strain the broth through a fine-mesh strainer and discard the solids.

2. Meanwhile, in a large bowl, mix together the matzah ball mix, eggs, vegetable oil, schmaltz, dill, parsley, chicken consommé powder, and seltzer. Let sit for 15 minutes.

3. Bring a large pot of salted water to a boil over high heat. Divide the matzah ball mixture into 12 balls about the size of walnuts. Put all the balls in the boiling water. Cover the pot, reduce the heat, and simmer for 25 minutes. Add the carrots and boil for 5 minutes, or until carrots are soft.

4. To serve, ladle the hot broth into bowls, add 2 matzah balls and several carrot coins, and garnish with dill.

Three Sisters Soup with Fry Bread

MARIA

Corn, beans, and squash are staples for Indigenous peoples all across North America. While I do not come from a corn culture, I have learned about these wonderful foods through my travels across Indian Country. They are often termed the "three sisters," and we eat them together because we grow them together: Corn grows tall so beans can climb the stalks, squash grows wide to protect corn and beans from predators, and beans fertilize the soil so corn and squash can grow. They work well together, just as their flavors do in this dish. Paired with fry bread, this dish tastes like a Native get-together! It's an easy meal that celebrates the land and the people who have tended it for millennia. It can easily be made vegetarian or vegan by swapping the chicken broth for vegetable broth in the soup and using nondairy milk to make the fry bread. **Serves 6**

1. Heat a cast iron grill pan or skillet over medium-high heat. Brush the corn with a little olive oil. Grill the corn until some char marks appear on all sides and the corn takes on a little color, 5–8 minutes. Transfer to a plate and set aside to cool. When cool enough to handle, stand each ear over a shallow bowl and use a sharp knife to remove the kernels from the cob.

2. Heat an Instant Pot on sauté mode, then add the olive oil and onion and cook until translucent, about 5 minutes. Add the chicken broth, corn, and beans. Close the lid and set to sealing. Cook at high pressure for 40 minutes. Allow the pressure to release naturally for 10 minutes, then release the remaining pressure.

3. Add the butternut squash and seal the lid again. Pressure cook for 5 minutes, then allow the pressure to release naturally. Remove the lid and taste the soup; season with salt and pepper as desired.

4. Ladle into bowls and top with green chiles if you like.

★ Fry Bread ★

4 cups all-purpose flour

2½ tablespoons baking powder

1 teaspoon salt

1 teaspoon sugar

1½ cups milk

1 tablespoon vegetable oil, plus more for frying

1. In a large bowl, whisk together the flour, baking powder, salt, and sugar.

2. Heat the milk in a small saucepan over medium heat. When warm, add to the flour mixture, then add the oil. Mix the dough with your hands until smooth. Place the dough in a lightly greased bowl, cover with a damp clean kitchen towel, and allow to rise for 1 hour.

3. In a large skillet with high sides, heat 1 inch oil over medium heat to 375 degreeS F. To test the heat, add a small piece of dough to the oil; it should puff up. Shape the dough into 4-inch squares. Working in batches, fry the dough, flipping until golden brown all over, 3–4 minutes. Transfer to paper towels to drain.

4 ears corn, husked and cleaned

2 teaspoons olive oil, plus more for brushing

1 onion, diced

2 quarts chicken broth

1 cup dried tepary beans (see note), soaked overnight and drained

1 butternut squash, peeled, seeded, and cut into 1-inch cubes

Salt and ground black pepper to taste

1 (4-ounce) can green chiles, drained (optional)

Note: Tepary beans are small heirloom varieties that Native people in the American Southwest have grown for generations. You can buy them online from Ramona Farms. You may substitute another dried bean of your choosing, though you may need to adjust the cooking time.

Salmorejo

Spanish Chilled Tomato Soup

ALEJANDRA

I fell in love with salmorejo, a creamy chilled tomato soup, while traveling around southern Spain a few summers ago. Salmorejo is similar in flavor to gazpacho, but the texture is thick, creamy, and absolutely luscious. The thickness comes from the addition of toasted bread, which absorbs excess liquid and thickens the pureed tomatoes. Smoked paprika and garlic add depth and a hint of spice. Served with fun garnishes like jamon serrano, chorizo, or chopped boiled egg, it's filling while still feeling cool and refreshing—a perfect meal for sweltering summer afternoons no matter where you are! **Serves 4–6**

1. Place a fine-mesh strainer over a bowl. Cut the tomatoes in half and squeeze over the strainer in order to remove the seeds. Set the squeezed tomatoes aside. Use a spoon to press the seeds in the strainer to extract as much liquid as possible. Discard the seeds, but reserve the liquid in the bowl.

2. Combine the toasted bread, almonds, and garlic in a blender and process until coarsely chopped. Add the squeezed tomatoes, reserved tomato liquid, vinegar, paprika, and red pepper flakes (if using) and puree until very smooth. (Do this in batches if you don't have a very powerful blender.) Add the salt and olive oil and puree again. The texture should be thick and creamy, but smooth—similar to a butternut squash soup. If yours is too thick, add a bit of water. If too thin, add a bit more toasted bread. Taste and adjust the seasoning with additional salt, if desired.

3. Transfer the salmorejo to a bowl, cover, and chill for at least 2 hours, until very cold. Serve topped with chopped egg and serrano ham, chorizo, or bacon.

3½ pounds ripe tomatoes

1½ cups chopped toasted sandwich bread (3–4 slices)

½ cup whole almonds

5 large garlic cloves, peeled

2 teaspoons sherry vinegar

1 teaspoon smoked Spanish paprika

½ teaspoon red pepper flakes (optional)

1 teaspoon kosher salt, plus more to taste

½ cup extra-virgin olive oil

1 hard-boiled egg, peeled and chopped

½ cup chopped serrano ham, cured chorizo, or crisp bacon

Handhelds

Dan Dan Sliders with Cucumber Salad

ABBE

With a husband who worked in China for many years and a son who lived there, I grew to appreciate the flavors of Szechuan cooking. Now, Szechuan peppercorns, with their numbing effect and spicy flavor, are always in my spice cabinet. We love dan dan noodles, but one day, not having noodles on hand, I decided to serve the ground pork on buns instead, and a family fave was created. These ground pork sliders are almost like a sloppy Joe, but with the iconic flavor of Szechuan peanut sauce. They're a quick way to get dinner on the table—and they're spicy, so you'll love the cooling cucumber salad on the side. **Serves 6**

1. Heat the oil in a large skillet over medium heat. Add the pork and cook, stirring and breaking up the meat into bite-size chunks, until just pink, about 8 minutes. Add the ginger and garlic and continue to cook until the pork is light brown, 5–8 minutes. Add the stock, chili garlic sauce, vinegar, soy, tahini, sugar, and Szechuan peppercorns. Cook until thickened, 7–10 minutes. Stir in the peanut butter.

2. Meanwhile, brush the buns with chili oil and toast them.

3. Spoon the pork between the toasted buns. Sprinkle with the scallions and peanuts and serve with cucumber salad (below).

1 tablespoon vegetable oil

2 pounds ground pork

¼ cup chopped peeled ginger

2 tablespoons chopped garlic

1½ cups chicken stock

¼ cup chili garlic sauce

¼ cup red wine vinegar

¼ cup soy sauce

3 tablespoons tahini

1 teaspoon brown sugar

2 teaspoons cracked Szechuan peppercorns

2–4 tablespoons peanut butter

12 slider buns, split

2 teaspoons chili oil

8 scallions, thinly sliced

½ cup chopped salted peanuts

★ Cucumber Salad ★

2 tablespoons Chinkiang vinegar or rice vinegar

2 teaspoons chili oil

2 teaspoons toasted sesame oil

2 teaspoons turbinado sugar or brown sugar

½ teaspoon kosher salt

6 mini cucumbers or 2 English cucumbers

2 teaspoons sesame seeds

¼ cup chopped salted peanuts

¼ cup fresh cilantro leaves

1. In a medium bowl, whisk together the vinegar, chili oil, sesame oil, sugar, and salt until the sugar dissolves.

2. Halve the cucumbers lengthwise and scoop out the seeds if they are seedy. Place the cucumbers cut side down on a cutting board and lightly smash them with a cleaver or chef's knife until they crack in a few places. Slice into ¾-inch half-moons.

3. Toss the cucumbers in the dressing and top with the sesame seeds, peanuts, and cilantro.

Carne Asada Tacos with Tomato and Tomatillo Salsas

MARIA

Everyone loves tacos, but these are my absolute favorite. Beware, you might smoke out the kitchen with the high heat and marinade on these guys! But it will be well worth it in the end. The key to this recipe is the salsas (yes, two salsas: tomato and tomatillo) and the marinade. Both salsas require charring some ingredients to release the flavor before blending them. I also include chicken bouillon in the green salsa to add depth of flavor. In the marinade, I always use orange juice for a little added sugar to caramelize the outside of the meat. These steps are critical for making good tacos taste great. **Serves 6**

Beef and salsas

Juice of 3 limes, divided

1 cup orange juice

1–2 tablespoons soy sauce, or to taste

1 head garlic, cloves separated and peeled

1½ pounds flank steak, cut against the grain into ¼- to ½-inch strips

10 serrano peppers

4 tomatoes

3 white onions, peeled

5 tomatillos, husked

2 bunches cilantro

10 jalapeño peppers

To serve

12 corn tortillas

Crumbled cotija cheese

Chopped white onion

Fresh cilantro leaves

Sour cream

1. In a medium bowl, mix half of the lime juice, the orange juice, and soy sauce together. Crush 3 garlic cloves and add them to the marinade. Add the beef, toss to coat, and let it sit for 20 minutes.

2. While the beef is marinating, make the salsas. Preheat the broiler and line a cast iron skillet with aluminum foil.

3. Working in batches, put the serranos, tomatoes, onions, and tomatillos in the prepared skillet and broil until they are blackened in spots, watching carefully and turning occasionally to char all sides.

4. For the tomato salsa, transfer the tomatoes, 1 onion, 1 bunch cilantro, 5 garlic cloves, the jalapeños, and the remaining lime juice to a blender. Puree until the mixture is slightly chunky. Transfer to a bowl and set aside or chill until ready to serve.

5. For the tomatillo salsa, combine the tomatillos, serranos, remaining 1 bunch cilantro, remaining 2 onions, and remaining garlic cloves in the blender (no need to wash the blender between salsas). Puree until the mixture is slightly chunky. Transfer to a bowl and set aside or chill until ready to use.

6. Grease a grill pan and heat over high heat. Remove the beef from the marinade and grill for about 3 minutes on each side. Transfer to a plate.

7. In a large cast iron skillet, toast the tortillas over medium-high heat until lightly charred, flipping once, 1–2 minutes on each side.

8. To serve, fill the tortillas with beef and top with cheese. Garnish with chopped onion, cilantro, sour cream, and salsas.

Cleveland Polish Boy and Pierogies

MIKE

In Cleveland, Ohio, there are so many pockets of diversity in a five-mile radius that it is practically impossible not to be immersed in different culinary experiences. Two things that are extremely "Cleveland" are pierogies and Polish boys.

Pierogies are a way of life in Cleveland and enjoyed from Lenten season all the way until the fall and winter months. Pierogies can be stuffed with literally anything—potatoes, onions, cream cheese, sweet fillings—and they are always filled with love.

In addition to pierogies, when you come to Cleveland, you have to have a Polish boy sausage sandwich. Saucy, sweet, messy, delicious: These are all the words that describe a true Polish boy and give you a wonderful glimpse into what Cleveland has to offer. A Polish boy is meant to be messy and to fill you with an unmatched level of comfort. Every Polish boy that you have in Cleveland is different, but they all have the same basic ingredients: sausage in a bun, covered with a layer of french fries, coleslaw, and barbecue sauce. And once again, if it's not cooked with love, don't eat it. **Serves 6**

Sandwiches

6 all-beef Polish sausages, preferably Scott Pete

6 hoagie rolls without sesame seeds, split

1 cup ketchup- and vinegar-based barbecue sauce

French fries

2 russet potatoes, peeled and cut into fries

3 cups vegetable oil

Slaw

1 cup sugar

1 cup heavy cream

1 cup mayonnaise

½ head purple cabbage, thinly sliced

½ head green cabbage, thinly sliced

1 carrot, shredded

Salt to taste

1. Bring a large pot of water to a boil over high heat. Add the sausages and cook for 15 minutes. Turn off the heat and leave the sausages in the hot water until ready to build the sandwiches.

2. To make the french fries, fill a large bowl with ice water and add the fries; this will rinse off some of the starch. Drain the fries on a clean kitchen towel.

3. In a large skillet or heavy pot, heat the oil over medium heat to 350 degrees F. Set a wire rack over a rimmed baking sheet. Add the fries to the hot oil and cook until golden brown, flipping and stirring occasionally for even frying, about 12 minutes. Transfer the fries to the rack.

4. Meanwhile, to make the coleslaw, in a large bowl, combine the sugar, cream, and mayonnaise and mix until evenly incorporated. Add the cabbages and carrot and stir to coat evenly. Season with salt.

5. To serve, remove the sausages from the hot water and place one in each hoagie roll. Top with a pile of coleslaw and some french fries, then drizzle with barbecue sauce. Serve with pierogies (recipe follows).

(recipe continues)

★ Sausage Pierogies with Barbecue Crema ★

Pierogies (makes extra filling)

4 tablespoons (½ stick) unsalted butter, divided

2 tablespoons olive oil

3 all-beef Polish sausages, preferably Scott Pete, skin removed and diced

½ head purple cabbage, diced

½ head green cabbage, diced

1 russet potato, peeled and diced

1 onion, diced

2 cups all-purpose flour, plus more for dusting

1 large egg

½ cup hot water

1 teaspoon salt, plus more for seasoning

Pinch ground black pepper

Pinch paprika

Pinch seasoned salt, preferably Lawry's

Barbecue crema

¼–½ cup ketchup- and vinegar-based barbecue sauce

1 cup sour cream

Pinch paprika

1. To make the pierogi filling, melt 2 tablespoons of the butter with the olive oil in a large sauté pan over medium-high heat. Add the sausage, cabbages, potato, and onion and cook, stirring, until the potato and cabbages are tender, 8–10 minutes. Transfer the filling to a bowl to cool.

2. To make the pierogi dough, combine the flour, egg, hot water, salt, pepper, paprika, and seasoned salt in a food processor. Process until the dough lifts from the edges of the bowl and starts to form a ball. Transfer the dough ball to a bowl, cover with plastic wrap, and refrigerate for 20 minutes.

3. Bring a large pot of water to a boil over high heat.

4. While the water is coming to a boil, roll out the dough on a floured surface to about ⅛ inch thick. Use a 3- or 4-inch round biscuit cutter or a sharp knife to out circles of dough. You should get about 14 circles. Working with one dough circle at a time, place about 1 tablespoon filling in the middle of the circle. Using a pastry brush or your finger, dab a tiny bit of water on the edge of the dough, then fold the dough over onto itself to form a half-moon shape. Crimp the edge with a fork. Repeat to form all the pierogies.

5. Salt the boiling water, then gently add the pierogis to the pot. Boil for about 5 minutes; the pierogis will float to the surface when done. Drain the pierogies.

6. Heat the remaining 2 tablespoons butter in a sauté pan over medium heat. Add the pierogies and cook until nicely browned and crispy on both sides, 2–4 minutes. Remove from the pan and drain on paper towels.

7. To make the barbecue crema, in a small bowl, whisk together the barbecue sauce, sour cream, and paprika until smooth.

8. Serve the pierogies with the barbecue crema.

Schnitzel Sandwich with Fried Eggplant & Matbucha in a Brioche

BRAD

This is the sandwich you didn't know you needed. This meal is something you would easily find in the shuk (outdoor market) in Israel and is a traditional Friday lunch meal among Israelis. Each component of this dish is wonderful on its own, but when the crispy schnitzel, smoky eggplant, and spicy tomato matbucha sauce come together on a tender brioche bun, it's just an unbeatable and truly delicious combination. **Serves 6**

Matbucha

1–2 tablespoons olive oil

8 long hot peppers, thinly sliced

3 jalapeño peppers, thinly sliced

1 head garlic, cloves separated, peeled, and thinly sliced

1 (28-ounce) can whole peeled San Marzano tomatoes

2 tablespoons sweet paprika

2 tablespoons hot paprika

Kosher salt to taste

Chicken and eggplant

2 cups all-purpose flour

2 large eggs, beaten

2 cups bread crumbs

½ cup white sesame seeds

12 thin chicken breast cutlets

1 tablespoon kosher salt, plus more for sprinkling

½ teaspoon ground black pepper

2 cups vegetable oil

2 eggplants, trimmed and thinly sliced crosswise

Sandwiches

1 cup hummus, store-bought or homemade (page 91)

6 brioche rolls, split and toasted

6 Israeli pickles, sliced lengthwise

½ cup chopped fresh parsley

6 long peppers (optional)

1. To make the matbucha, in a large saucepan, heat the oil over medium heat. Add the hot peppers, jalapeños, and garlic and sauté for 5 minutes. Add the tomatoes with their juices and let simmer until thick, 15–20 minutes. Add both paprikas and season with salt.

2. To make the chicken and eggplant, prepare three bowls for breading: one with the flour; one with the eggs; and one with the bread crumbs and sesame seeds, mixed. Season the chicken cutlets all over with the salt and pepper. Dredge each piece of chicken in the flour, then in the egg, and then in the sesame bread crumbs.

3. Heat the oil in a large skillet over medium heat until a bread crumb dropped in the oil sizzles. Working in batches, fry the chicken until golden and cooked through, about 5 minutes on each side. Transfer to a plate lined with paper towels. Leave the heat on under the skillet.

4. While the chicken is cooking, line a rimmed baking sheet with paper towels and set a wire rack on top. Place the eggplant slices on the rack, sprinkle with kosher salt, and allow to sit for 5 minutes. Pat the eggplant dry, then fry until golden brown, about 3 minutes per side. Return the eggplant slices to the rack to drain.

5. To assemble the sandwiches, spread the hummus on the bottom half of each brioche roll. Top with some of the pickles. Add a few slices of eggplant and then a chicken cutlet. Top with some parsley. Spread the matbucha on the top half of each roll and close the sandwiches. Serve hot, with a long pepper alongside, if you like.

Fried Fish Sandwiches and Tostones

You can't go to Barbados without having a few pieces of fried flying fish and plantain. One of my favorite ways to enjoy flying fish is on a salt bread roll with a little Bajan "peppa sauce" on top and a side of tostones. Now, flying fish is pretty hard to come by in America, so any fresh, flaky white fish will do for this recipe—on *The Great American Recipe* I made it with catfish. As for the plantain, well, plantain is the gift that just keeps on giving. You can fry it, boil it, roast it, bake it . . . no matter how you make it, it is always delicious, but tostones are one of my favorite ways to have green plantain. Just give the recipe a try and you will see why. **Serves 12**

1. Put the catfish in a large bowl and sprinkle it with the salt and lime juice. Gently roll the catfish in the lime and salt, cover the bowl with plastic wrap, and place it in the refrigerator until you're ready to cook.

2. To make the pepper sauce, put on food-safe gloves to protect your skin. Remove the stems from the peppers and put the peppers in a food processor. Add the onion and pulse until the mixture is paste-like. Add the turmeric, mustard, oil, and vinegar and process until smooth, stopping to scrape down the sides of the bowl occasionally so that everything gets mixed in evenly. Pour the pepper sauce into a small saucepan and set over medium-low heat. Slowly add a little bit of water until you get the desired consistency. Bring the pepper sauce to a simmer.

3. While the pepper sauce simmers, prepare the fish. Combine the onion powder, garlic powder, paprika, black and white peppers, and dried parsley in a small bowl and mix well. Set aside.

4. In a large bowl, whisk together the eggs until well blended. Set aside.

5. Put the flour in a second large bowl and season it with a little salt and white pepper. Set aside.

6. Take the fish out of the refrigerator, rinse it off, and pat it dry. Season the fillets all over with the seasoning mixture, then dredge first in the egg and then in the seasoned flour.

7. In a large, deep skillet, heat about ½ inch oil over medium heat to 350–375 degrees F. Set a wire rack over a rimmed baking sheet.

8. Working in batches, fry the catfish, flipping the fillets over to make sure both sides are fried to a deep golden brown, about 4 minutes on each side. Transfer the catfish to the wire rack to drain.

9. While the catfish are frying, butter and toast the brioche buns.

10. To serve, place some lettuce and tomato on the bottom of each bun, top with a piece of fish, and slather some mayo and pepper sauce on the top of the bun; close the sandwiches.

11. Serve warm with tostones (recipe follows).

Sandwiches

6 catfish fillets, cut in half

1 tablespoon iodized salt, plus more for seasoning

Juice of 3 limes

2 teaspoons onion powder

2 teaspoons garlic powder

2 teaspoons smoked paprika

2 teaspoons ground black pepper

1 teaspoon ground white pepper, plus more for seasoning

2 teaspoons dried parsley

4 large eggs

2 cups all-purpose flour

Vegetable oil, for frying

2 tablespoons unsalted butter, softened

12 brioche buns, split

1 head lettuce romaine or iceberg lettuce, shredded

1 large beefsteak tomato, sliced

¼ cup mayonnaise

Pepper sauce

8–10 Scotch bonnet peppers

1 small Vidalia onion, roughly chopped

1 teaspoon ground turmeric

2 tablespoons yellow mustard

1 tablespoon vegetable oil

½ cup white vinegar

½ cup water, or more as needed

(recipe continues)

★ Tostones ★

4 green plantains
Vegetable oil, for frying
Sea salt, for serving
Lime juice, for serving

1. Cut off the ends of each plantain, then slice the skin down the middle. Peel the plantains and cut into rounds that are about ½ inch thick.

2. In a large pot, bring 3 quarts water to a boil over high heat. Add the plantains and boil until tender, 12–15 minutes. Drain and let cool slightly.

3. Place a plantain round on a long sheet of parchment paper, then fold the paper over so that the plantain is sandwiched in between. Using a heavy jar or can, gently flatten the plantain to about ¼ inch thick. Be careful not to make it too thin. Repeat with all the plantain rounds.

4. In a large skillet, heat about ½ inch oil over medium heat to 350–375 degrees F. Working in batches, fry the plantains until golden brown, flipping halfway through, 6–8 minutes total. Transfer to paper towels to drain. Sprinkle with salt and lime juice and serve with pepper sauce.

Gyro Pitas

TED

Gyro is a classic Greek sandwich stuffed with slices of meat cooked on a vertical rotisserie. The meat is sliced thin off the rotisserie and served in a warm pita with tomatoes, onions, and sauce. Since most of us do not have a vertical rotisserie at home, I prepare a ground lamb and beef mixture with a variety of spices and put it on a skewer to grill. I then slide the cooked meat off the skewer and serve it in a warm pita, which makes it a perfect dish to enjoy at home or on the go. **Serves 6**

1. In a large bowl, combine the lamb, beef, onion powder, garlic powder, chicken base, beef base, oregano, cumin, cloves, salt, and pepper. Using your hands or an electric mixer fitted with the paddle attachment, mix the meat mixture until the spices are thoroughly combined. Place the bowl in the refrigerator for 10 minutes.

2. While the meat mixture is chilling, make the white sauce. In a medium bowl, whisk together the yogurt, mayonnaise, lemon juice, and garlic. Whisk until the sauce is well mixed, thinning the mixture, if necessary, with water. It should be the consistency of maple syrup. Place the bowl in the refrigerator until ready to serve.

3. Heat a large grill pan over medium-high heat. Divide the meat mixture into 6 portions. Press the meat into a cylinder around each of 6 metal skewers. Grill the skewers until the meat is cooked through, 10–12 minutes, turning to brown all sides.

4. Transfer the skewers to a platter and let rest for a minute or two. Slide the meat from each skewer into a pita, then top with tomato and onion slices and drizzle with white sauce. Wrap the gyros in aluminum foil and sprinkle with cayenne pepper and chopped parsley. Serve immediately.

Lamb and beef

1 pound ground lamb

1 pound ground beef

2 tablespoons onion powder

2 tablespoons garlic powder

2 tablespoons chicken base

2 tablespoons beef base

2 tablespoons dried Greek oregano

1 tablespoon ground cumin

½ teaspoon ground cloves

1 teaspoon salt

1 teaspoon ground black pepper

White sauce

1 cup full-fat Greek yogurt

¼ cup mayonnaise

Juice of ½ lemon

1 garlic clove, minced

Water (if needed)

To serve

6 pitas

3 Roma tomatoes, sliced

1 red onion, sliced

Pinch cayenne pepper

Chopped fresh parsley

Mini Spinach B'jíbín Pies

BRAD

I grew up in a predominantly Syrian Jewish community, and it has certainly impacted my palate. These mini spinach pies are my take on a Syrian Jewish classic dish that I've been eating since I was a child. B'jíbín is traditionally served in large trays and cut into squares. These mini b'jíbín are perfect for easy grab-and-go snacks, a brunch, or a dairy holiday meal. They are easy to make and so delicious, because how can you go wrong with spinach and cheese pies? **Makes 12 mini pies**

1. Preheat the oven to 400 degrees F. Grease a 12-cup muffin tin.

2. In a large bowl, mix together the flour, 1 teaspoon of the salt, the sugar, and baking powder. Mix in ½ cup of the oil and the cold water until uniform in texture. Divide the dough into 12 equal balls. Place a dough ball in each prepared muffin cup. Press the dough into the bottom and up the sides to form a mini crust.

3. In a small skillet, heat the remaining 1 tablespoon oil over medium heat. Add the onion and sauté until soft, about 5 minutes.

4. In a large bowl, whisk the eggs together. Add the spinach, cooked onion, all the cheeses, consommé powder, garlic powder, remaining 1 teaspoon salt, the black pepper, and cayenne and mix thoroughly. Divide the spinach mixture equally into the mini crusts. Bake for 30–40 minutes, until cooked through. Serve warm or at room temperature.

2 cups all-purpose flour

2 teaspoons kosher salt, divided

1 teaspoon sugar

1 teaspoon baking powder

½ cup plus 1 tablespoon vegetable oil

¼ cup cold water

1 onion, chopped

4 large eggs

2 pounds frozen chopped spinach, thawed and squeezed dry

½ cup shredded mozzarella cheese

½ cup ricotta cheese

½ cup crumbled feta cheese

½ cup shredded Muenster cheese

¼ cup grated Parmesan cheese

1 teaspoon chicken consommé powder

1 teaspoon garlic powder

½ teaspoon ground black pepper

Pinch cayenne pepper

Croque Madame Mini Quiches and Dijon Béchamel with Fruit Salad

KHELA

These mini quiches are a play on a favorite brunch item, the croque madame. I take the key flavors of ham and cheese and use puff pastry as the "bread" to turn them into mini quiches. The best part, though, is the béchamel. Dijon is perfect in the creamy sauce. For a variation, you can add cheese, turning it into a delicious Mornay sauce. For color, texture, and a hit of acid, a salad is great as a side. The sweetness and tangy qualities of this fruit salad lend brightness and complement the richness of the eggs. **Makes 9 mini quiches**

1. Preheat the oven to 400 degrees F. Spray a 12-cup muffin tin with nonstick cooking spray.

2. On a lightly floured surface, roll out the puff pastry sheet to about ¼ inch thick. Cut it into 9 squares. Press the pastry squares into the prepared muffin cups. Bake for 5 minutes.

3. Meanwhile, heat the oil in a large skillet over medium heat. Add the onion and sauté until soft, about 5 minutes. Add the garlic and sauté until the garlic is soft, about 2 minutes. Remove the pan from the heat.

4. In a small bowl, make an egg wash by whisking together 2 of the eggs and 2 tablespoons of the cream.

5. In a large bowl, whisk together the remaining 4 eggs and remaining cream until well blended. Add the nutmeg and season with salt and pepper.

6. Fill each of the pastry-lined muffin cups with equal amounts of the ham, cheese, cooked onion and garlic, thyme, and chives, then pour over the egg and cream mixture. Brush the edges of the dough with the egg wash. Bake for 15–18 minutes, until the pastry is golden brown and the egg mixture is set. Let cool slightly before serving.

7. While the mini quiches bake, make the Dijon béchamel. In a small skillet, melt the butter over medium heat. Add the garlic and cook for 1 minute. Whisk in the flour to make a roux. Cook the roux for several minutes, stirring constantly, until it takes on a light brown color. Slowly add the milk, whisking constantly, until you have a thickened and smooth sauce. Add the nutmeg and Dijon mustard and stir to fully incorporate. Taste the sauce and season with salt and pepper as needed.

8. Pour the béchamel over the mini quiches and serve with fruit salad (recipe follows).

Croque madame mini quiches

All-purpose flour, for dusting

1 sheet frozen puff pastry, thawed

1 tablespoon olive oil or unsalted butter

½ small sweet onion, diced

1 garlic clove, grated

6 large eggs

¾ cup heavy cream, divided

¼ teaspoon freshly grated nutmeg

Salt and ground black pepper to taste

4 ounces ham, diced

1½ cups shredded Gruyère cheese

1 tablespoon fresh thyme

2 tablespoons chopped fresh chives

Dijon béchamel

1 tablespoon unsalted butter

1 small garlic clove, grated

1 tablespoon all-purpose flour

¾ cup whole milk

¼ teaspoon freshly grated nutmeg

1½ teaspoons Dijon mustard

Salt and pepper to taste

★ Fruit Salad ★

1 bunch red grapes

1 bunch green grapes

1 large or 2 small Pink Lady or Fuji apples, cored and sliced

1 large or 2 small pears, cored and sliced

⅓ cup dried cranberries

1½ tablespoons honey

1 tablespoon orange juice

1½ teaspoons fresh lime juice

Maldon salt, for finishing

1. Combine the grapes, apples, pears, and cranberries in a large bowl.

2. In a small bowl, mix together the honey, orange juice, and lime juice until the honey is dissolved. Pour the juice mixture over the fruit. Stir gently to evenly incorporate the dressing. Sprinkle with a tiny bit of Maldon salt right before serving.

Prosciutto Egg Cups

TED

My family and I lived in a loft in the city for years and always loved throwing parties and entertaining. When we were ready to move into a house, I was fortunate as an architect to be able to design and build our dream home. I wanted to still be able to make great meals and great memories for my friends and family in our new space. Brunch is one of my favorite ways to entertain, and I made this dish for one of the first gatherings in our new home: Salty prosciutto is formed into cups to hold a filling of veggies and egg, then baked until the shell is crispy and the egg is set. **Makes 12 egg cups; serves 6**

4 tablespoons (½ stick) unsalted butter, softened

1 tablespoon Greek olive oil

2 garlic cloves, grated

5 cups baby spinach, roughly chopped

1½ cups finely chopped roasted red peppers

24 very thin slices prosciutto

12 large eggs

Salt and ground black pepper to taste

1 (½-ounce) package fresh chives, minced

6 slices sourdough bread, toasted

1. Preheat the oven to 450 degrees F. Spread the butter in the cups of a 12-cup muffin tin.

2. Heat the oil in a large skillet over medium heat. Add the garlic and sauté for 1 minute. Add the spinach, cover the pan, and cook until the spinach is wilted. Add the roasted red peppers and sauté for 1 minute. Transfer the mixture to a strainer and drain off the excess liquid.

3. Layer each prepared muffin cup with 2 slices prosciutto, creating a cup shape. Divide the spinach mixture evenly among the cups.

4. Crack an egg into each cup. Add a pinch of salt and pepper on the egg.

5. Bake for 10–15 minutes. Allow to cool for 5 minutes, then gently remove the egg cups from the muffin tin. Garnish with the chives. Serve 2 egg cups to each person with 1 slice toast, cut into 2 triangles.

Citrus–Maple Glazed Pork Steak Wrap with Kohlrabi and Fennel

KHELA

My family loves pork and I love a good salad. This wrap is a perfect marriage of the two. The good thing about pork steaks is they are forgiving like chicken thighs and don't dry out as easily as pork chops or pork loin cuts. The kohlrabi has a nice mild flavor and texture that complements the stronger notes of the fennel and radish. These veggies, with the citrus-mint dressing, offer a crunch and freshness to the wrap that can't be beat. Optionally, you can do double duty by serving the sweet and savory pork for dinner and then using the leftovers in a wrap for a quick on-the-go meal. **Serves 4–6**

Orange-maple pork

2 cups orange juice

Juice of 2 limes

½ cup maple syrup

4 garlic cloves, grated

2 teaspoons onion powder

Pinch red pepper flakes

3 boneless pork shoulder steaks,
    1½ inches thick

2 tablespoons unsalted butter

Salt and ground black pepper to taste

4–6 large flour tortillas or thin flatbread wraps

Veggies

Grated zest and juice of ½ orange

¼ cup extra virgin olive oil

½ garlic clove, grated

Salt and ground black pepper to taste

3 cups shredded lettuce, such as
    romaine or curly leaf

1 small kohlrabi, peeled and cut into
    julienne

1 small fennel bulb, trimmed
    and thinly sliced

4 radishes, thinly sliced

⅓ small red onion, thinly sliced

2 tablespoons chopped fresh mint

Maldon salt (optional)

Dijon-maple yogurt spread

½ cup full-fat Greek yogurt

2 tablespoons Dijon mustard

1 tablespoon maple syrup

1. To make the pork, in a medium bowl, whisk together the orange juice, lime juice, maple syrup, garlic, onion powder, and red pepper flakes. Divide the mixture in half. Put one half in a very large plastic zipper-top bag, add the pork shoulder steaks, and marinate for 15–60 minutes. Put the other half, along with the butter, in a small saucepan and heat over medium-high heat until reduced, about 10 minutes.

2. Preheat a grill to high heat.

3. Remove the pork shoulder steaks from the marinade (discard the marinade). Liberally salt and pepper both sides. Brush the steaks on both sides with the reduced orange and maple mixture. Grill the steaks until they reach 145 degrees F, 6–8 minutes per side. Set aside to let them rest.

4. While the pork steaks rest, prepare the veggies. In a small bowl, whisk together the orange zest and juice, olive oil, garlic, salt, and pepper. In a large bowl, combine the lettuce, kohlrabi, fennel, radishes, red onion, and mint. Toss in the dressing a little at a time until most of the veggies are very lightly glistening. You want it only lightly dressed so you don't end up with a soggy wrap. Finish the veggie mixture with a tiny sprinkle of Maldon, if you like.

5. To make the Dijon-maple spread, in a small bowl, whisk together the yogurt, Dijon mustard, and maple syrup.

6. Thinly slice the pork steaks against the grain. To assemble the wraps, spread each tortilla with the Dijon-maple spread, leaving 1 inch bare around the edges. Add about ½ cup of the veggie mixture to the center of each wrap. Top with about 4 ounces sliced pork. Fold the bottom of the wrap over the vegetables and pork, then fold both sides up and roll the bundle away from you, sealing the wrap. Wrap each wrap in aluminum foil and cut in half before serving.

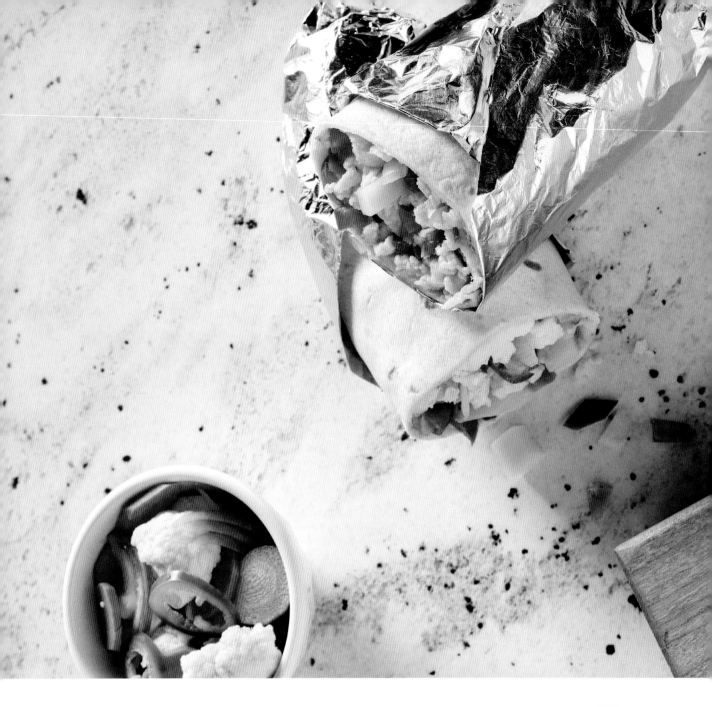

Grab-and-Go Breakfast Burritos

ABBE

With twins who skied every weekend with their dad, I needed something to send with them for breakfast in the car or a late afternoon snack. These breakfast burritos with a scrambled egg, veggie, and potato filling have been their favorite for many, many years. They are perfect for keeping in the freezer and taking out when needed—which really could be every day. **Serves 8**

Pickled veggies escabeche

1 small Bermuda onion, peeled and thinly sliced

2 carrots, peeled and thinly sliced

1 jalapeño pepper, sliced into rings

½ cup small cauliflower florets

¾ cup water

¾ cup white vinegar or apple cider vinegar

3 tablespoons sugar

1 tablespoon kosher salt

1 garlic clove, crushed

1 teaspoon dried oregano

Burritos

3 cups peeled and cubed russet potatoes

3 tablespoons vegetable oil

1¼ cups diced onion

1¼ cups diced red bell pepper

1½ cups chopped deli honey ham

2 (4-ounce) cans diced green chiles, drained, or 12 fresh Hatch chiles, diced

14 large eggs

⅓ cup milk

½ teaspoon salt

2 tablespoons unsalted butter

½ cup minced fresh cilantro

8 (10-inch) flour tortillas

2 cups shredded cheddar cheese

2 cups shredded jalapeño cheese

1. To make the pickled vegetables, in a large bowl, combine the onion, carrots, jalapeño, and cauliflower.

2. In a medium saucepan, combine the water, vinegar, sugar, salt, garlic, and oregano. Bring the mixture to a boil over high heat, then pour it over the vegetables in the bowl. Set aside until cooled to room temperature, then refrigerate until ready to serve.

3. To make the burritos, bring a medium saucepan of salted water to a boil over high heat. Add the potatoes and cook for about 10 minutes, until tender but not too soft. Drain and set aside to cool.

4. Heat the oil in a large nonstick skillet over medium-high heat. Add the onion, bell pepper, and potatoes and cook, stirring occasionally, until the potatoes start to turn golden. Stir in the ham and half of the green chiles and cook for 1 minute. Remove the pan from the heat.

5. In a large bowl, whisk together the eggs, milk, and salt until well mixed. Heat the butter in a large nonstick skillet over medium heat. (You may have to cook the eggs in two batches, depending on the size of your pan.) Add the eggs and cook, stirring constantly, until mostly set. Before the eggs are thoroughly cooked, stir in the remaining green chiles and the cilantro. Let the eggs cool.

6. Tear 8 large squares of aluminum foil. In a large, dry skillet, heat the tortillas one by one until they are pliable and easy to fold. Place each warmed tortilla on a square of foil. Top each tortilla with an equal amount of the cheeses, potato mixture, and egg mixture. Roll up the tortilla like an egg roll, then roll the burrito in the foil the same way. (The wrapped burritos can be frozen for future use. To reheat from frozen, remove the foil and rewrap the burrito in a paper towel. Heat in the microwave for 1–2 minutes, until warm throughout. Or leave the foil wrap on and reheat the burrito in the oven at 350 degrees F for 15 minutes.)

7. To serve, slice the burritos on the diagonal and serve with to-go cups of pickled vegetables.

Chicken Dinners

Baharat Chicken Thighs with Hummus and Flatbread

BRAD

This delicious and easy-to-cook cut of chicken is perfect for a quick weeknight meal. The chicken is simply seasoned with a mix of dry spices and can be cooked in under 15 minutes in your oven, toaster oven, or air fryer. The sautéed onions are a wonderful addition that elevates the dish while still keeping things quick and easy. Hummus pairs perfectly with the chicken and can be made in under 5 minutes. **Serves 6**

1. Preheat the oven to 450 degrees F.

2. Heat 1 tablespoon of the oil in a large cast iron skillet over medium heat. Add the onions and 1 teaspoon of the salt and sauté until soft, about 5 minutes. Transfer to a rimmed baking sheet.

3. Put the chicken in a large bowl and season all over with the baharat, remaining 1 teaspoon salt, black pepper, paprika, cayenne, and remaining 1 tablespoon oil. Marinate for 10 minutes.

4. Put the chicken on the baking sheet with the onions.

5. Roast the chicken and onions until the chicken is cooked through, about 15 minutes.

6. Serve the chicken with the hummus, flatbread (recipes follow), and Israeli pickles.

2 tablespoons extra virgin olive oil, preferably from Israel or California, divided

2 yellow onions, thinly sliced

2 teaspoons kosher salt, divided

6 boneless, skinless chicken thighs

2 tablespoons Libyan baharat spice

Ground black pepper, to taste

1 tablespoons paprika

1½ teaspoon cayenne pepper

Israeli pickles, for serving

★ Hummus ★

2 (15-ounce) cans Goya chickpeas, 1 can drained and 1 can undrained

⅔ cup tahini, preferably Baron's

4 garlic cloves, peeled

¼ cup lemon juice

⅓ cup olive oil, plus more for drizzling

1 teaspoon salt

1 tablespoon ground cumin

Paprika, for garnish

Chopped fresh parsley, for garnish

1. Combine the chickpeas, including the liquid from one of the cans, tahini, garlic, lemon juice, oil, salt, and cumin in a food processor and process until smooth, about 5 minutes. Taste and adjust the seasoning if needed. Garnish with paprika and chopped parsley and a drizzle of olive oil.

(recipe continues)

№ 2 | Flatbread

2 cups all-purpose flour,
   plus more for dusting

1½ teaspoons baking
   powder

¾ cup water

3 tablespoons olive oil

2 garlic cloves, minced

Chopped fresh dill,
   to taste

½ teaspoon salt

1. Preheat a cast iron skillet over medium-high heat.

2. In a large bowl, mix the flour, baking powder, and water. Add the oil, garlic, dill, and salt and mix well. Knead for 5 minutes.

3. Roll out the dough on a lightly floured work surface and form 6 mini flatbreads.

4. One at a time, cook the flatbreads in the skillet until lightly browned, about 1 minute on each side.

Drumsticks with Honey Soy Balsamic Glaze

LEANNA

I love my cast iron pans. Nothing gives a better sear! This recipe is the perfect way to put your cast iron skillet to use. The chicken is perfectly seasoned with a nice crispy skin in a sweet and tangy sauce that is so good, you'll want to lick your plate (and your fingers!) clean. **Serves 10**

1. Put the drumsticks in a large bowl. Drizzle the lime juice over the chicken, then sprinkle with salt and toss until the drumsticks are evenly coated with lime and salt. Be sure to rub some of the salt under the skin of each drumstick, too. Add some black pepper and garlic powder and toss to coat.

2. Pour oil into a large cast iron skillet to a depth of about 1 inch and heat over high heat to 350 degrees F. Add the chicken, skin side down, to the hot oil and reduce the heat to medium-high. Allow the skin to thoroughly brown before turning the chicken. Brown the chicken on all sides and allow to cook until the juices run clear (or 170 degrees F on a meat thermometer), about 20 minutes. Transfer the drumsticks to a paper towel–lined plate; reserve the oil in the skillet.

3. While the chicken is frying, in a small bowl, whisk together the balsamic vinegar, soy sauce, and honey. Set aside.

4. Add the shallots, sliced garlic, rosemary leaves, and peppercorns to the hot oil and fry for 1 minute. Add the honey-soy mixture. The sauce will bubble at first and then begin to thicken just a little. Stir occasionally and turn the heat down so the sauce is at a simmer.

5. Return the chicken to the skillet with the sauce. Use a spoon to ladle the sauce over the chicken. Allow the chicken to simmer in the sauce for 2–3 minutes. Transfer the chicken to a plate and serve immediately.

10 chicken drumsticks

Juice of 1 lime

Kosher salt and ground black pepper to taste

Garlic powder to taste

Vegetable oil, for frying

½ cup balsamic vinegar

¼ cup soy sauce

2 tablespoons honey

2 shallots, thinly sliced

2 garlic cloves, sliced

Leaves from 2 rosemary sprigs

1 teaspoon whole black peppercorns

Chicken Katsu with Edamame Rice

RELLE

As a busy working mom, I'm always looking for quick and easy dinner recipes. Chicken katsu with edamame rice is one of my go-tos. Breaded chicken fried to crispy perfection and served over a bed of edamame rice with a tangy tonkatsu sauce—what's not to love? **Serves 6**

Chicken katsu

Vegetable oil, for frying

1 cup all-purpose flour

1 teaspoon garlic salt

½ teaspoon ground black pepper

3 large eggs

2 cups panko bread crumbs

6 boneless, skinless chicken thighs

Tonkatsu sauce

½ cup ketchup

¼ cup Worcestershire sauce

1 tablespoon shoyu or soy sauce

1 tablespoon sugar

2 teaspoons mirin

1. Pour oil into a large, deep skillet to a depth of 1–2 inches. Heat the oil over medium-high heat to about 350 degrees F. Set a wire rack over a rimmed baking sheet.

2. While the oil is heating, dredge the chicken. In a shallow dish, whisk together the flour, garlic salt, and pepper. In a second shallow dish, beat the eggs. In a third shallow dish, put the panko. Working with one chicken thigh at a time, coat the chicken in the flour mixture, then shake off the excess flour. Dip the chicken in the beaten egg, being sure to cover the entire surface and letting the excess run off. Finally, dip the chicken in the panko, pressing the panko onto the chicken to coat evenly. Place the breaded chicken on a plate.

3. Add 3 chicken thighs to the hot oil and fry until golden brown, 10–15 minutes, flipping halfway through. Transfer the chicken to the rack to drain. Repeat with the remaining 3 chicken thighs. Let the chicken rest while making the tonkatsu sauce.

4. In a medium bowl, whisk together the ketchup, Worcestershire sauce, shoyu, sugar, and mirin.

5. Drizzle the tonkatsu sauce over the chicken or serve it on the side for dipping. Serve with edamame rice (recipe on the next page).

№ 2 | Edamame Rice

3 cups white rice

3 cups water

2¼ cups frozen shelled edamame

6 tablespoons ochazuke wakame furikake (wakame seaweed and rice cracker furikake mix)

3 tablespoons nametake (Japanese enoki mushroom topping)

1. Rinse the rice under cool running water until the water runs clear, then drain. Put the rice and water in a rice cooker and set to cook. This will take 15–20 minutes.

2. Meanwhile, bring a small pot of water to a rolling boil over high heat. Add the frozen edamame and cook until tender, 3–5 minutes. Drain.

3. After the rice is done cooking, let it cool for about 10 minutes. Then add the edamame, furikake, and nametake. Toss to combine.

Fried Chicken Tenders with Coleslaw

TED

My father, Tony, was born in Greece and as a young man traveled the world working on cargo ships. When he decided to make the US his permanent home, he immigrated to Birmingham, Alabama, where he could be close to extended family and friends. While the Greek family he was staying with made Greek dishes to make him feel at home, they also introduced him to fried chicken as a new comfort food in his new land.

My youngest daughter, Adelyn, never got to meet my father before he passed away, but chicken tenders are her favorite. This dish is just one way to connect my father to his granddaughter and pay homage to all of the extended family and friends in Birmingham who took him in and made him feel at home. **Serves 6**

Chicken tenders

Vegetable oil, for frying

6 large eggs

6 cups all-purpose flour

2 tablespoons kosher salt, plus more for seasoning

1 tablespoon ground white pepper

1 tablespoon smoked paprika

1 tablespoon garlic powder

1 tablespoon onion salt

2 teaspoons dry mustard

18 chicken tenderloins (or 6 boneless, skinless chicken breasts, cut into thirds)

Dipping sauce

½ cup mayonnaise

3 tablespoons honey

2 tablespoons barbecue sauce

2 teaspoons Dijon mustard

½ teaspoon ground mustard

Pinch paprika

1. Pour about 1 inch oil into a large, heavy pot and heat over medium-high heat to 350–375 degrees F. Set a wire rack over a rimmed baking sheet.

2. In a shallow dish, beat the eggs. In a second shallow dish, whisk together the flour, salt, white pepper, smoked paprika, garlic powder, onion salt, and mustard.

3. Working with one piece of chicken at a time, dip the chicken first in the beaten eggs, letting the excess drip off, then dredge in the flour mixture. Place the dredged chicken on a plate for 5 minutes to set up.

4. Add the chicken to the hot oil and fry until golden brown and cooked through (165 degrees F on a meat thermometer), about 10 minutes. Transfer the chicken to the rack to drain. Sprinkle with a pinch of salt.

5. While the chicken is frying, whisk together all the dipping sauce ingredients in a small bowl until well combined.

6. Serve the chicken tenders with the dipping sauce and coleslaw (below).

★ Coleslaw ★

1½ cups shredded green cabbage (about ½ head)

1 cup shredded purple cabbage (about ½ head)

3 large carrots, peeled and shredded

½ cup mayonnaise

1 tablespoon Dijon mustard

1½ teaspoons white wine vinegar

Splash apple cider vinegar

1 teaspoon sugar

2 pinches celery salt

Salt and ground black pepper to taste

1. Combine the cabbages and carrots in a large bowl. Add the mayonnaise, mustard, vinegars, sugar, and celery salt and toss to combine. Season with salt and pepper. Chill until ready to serve.

Chicken Chapli Kebabs with Yogurt Mint Sauce

SALMAH

Chicken chapli kebabs originate from the Mughals of northern Pakistan and are a popular street food throughout Southeast Asia. When most of us think of kebabs, skewered beef or lamb is what comes to mind, but chicken chapli kebabs are a little different—a difference that is described in the name. Chapli derives from the Pashto word for "flat." These patties are made of heavily spiced ground chicken, fried on all sides. The kebabs can be enjoyed on their own with an array of raw veggies and a yogurt mint sauce or rolled into warm pita or naan with lettuce and tomatoes. **Serves 10**

1. In a food processor, combine all the ingredients except the oil and pulse until just combined.

2. Form the mixture into 10 small patties, place on a plate, and refrigerate for 10 minutes.

3. Heat the oil in a large skillet over medium-high heat. Working in batches, fry the patties until cooked through, 5–8 minutes per side. Transfer the cooked patties to a wire rack to drain.

4. Serve with the yogurt mint sauce (below).

★ Yogurt Mint Sauce ★

1 cup plain yogurt
Juice of 1 lemon
¼ cup fresh cilantro
½ cup fresh mint
½ cucumber
1 green chile
Salt and ground black pepper to taste

1. Combine all the ingredients in a small food processor and blend until smooth.

1½ pounds ground chicken

1 small yellow onion, roughly chopped

5 garlic cloves, peeled

½-inch piece ginger

3 green chiles

1 tomato, roughly chopped

¼ cup roughly chopped fresh mint

¼ cup roughly chopped fresh cilantro

3 tablespoons pomegranate molasses

2 tablespoons ground cumin

4 teaspoons salt

4 teaspoons ground black pepper

1 tablespoon garam masala

1 tablespoon fennel seeds

1 teaspoon coriander seeds

3 tablespoons chickpea flour (besan)

1 large egg, beaten

2 tablespoons vegetable oil

Mama's Green Chile Chicken Enchiladas with Pico de Gallo

MARIA

My mom's green chile enchiladas were the first dish I learned how to make. I like to combine cheese, onions, and green chiles in the enchiladas to make sure each one has a dynamic flavor inside and out. This is one of my favorite weeknight meals that everyone from kids to elders loves. **Serves 10**

Chicken

4 boneless, skinless chicken breasts

Salt and ground black pepper to taste

Cayenne pepper to taste

Enchilada sauce

1 tablespoon olive oil

1 small white onion, chopped

2 serrano peppers, chopped

4 garlic cloves, minced

1 cup vegetable stock

1½ teaspoons ground cumin

1 teaspoon fine sea salt

½ teaspoon freshly ground black pepper

Enchiladas

Vegetable oil, for greasing

½ small yellow onion, diced

24 (6-inch) white corn tortillas

2 cups shredded cheddar cheese

5 (4-ounce) cans green chiles

1. Preheat the oven to 350 degrees F. Grease a 13 × 9-inch glass baking dish.

2. Season the chicken breasts all over with salt, black pepper, and cayenne. Place the chicken in the prepared baking dish and bake for 20 minutes, or until the chicken is cooked through. Remove from the oven and let cool. Once cool enough to handle, cut the chicken into 1-inch pieces.

3. While the chicken is cooking, make the enchilada sauce. Heat the olive oil in a large saucepan over medium heat. Add the onion, serrano peppers, and garlic and sauté until the vegetables are softened, about 8 minutes. Transfer the vegetable mixture to a blender, add the vegetable stock, cumin, salt, and pepper, and puree until smooth. Set aside.

4. To make the enchiladas, coat the bottom of a medium saucepan with vegetable oil and heat over medium-high heat. Add the onion and sauté until translucent, about 5 minutes. Remove from the heat and set aside.

5. Coat the bottom of a large cast iron skillet with oil and heat over medium heat. One or two at a time, soften the tortillas for 2–3 minutes per side. Wrap the softened tortillas in a clean towel as they are finished.

6. Set up an assembly line of the enchiladas, starting with the tortillas, then the enchilada sauce, chicken, cheese, green chiles, and onion. Have a clean cutting board or large serving plate to work on.

7. Coat the bottom of the cast iron skillet again with oil. Dip one tortilla in the enchilada sauce, covering the entire tortilla. Lay the soaked tortilla on your work surface, then add some chicken, cheese, green chiles, and onion. Roll up the tortilla and place it in the prepared cast iron skillet, seam side down. Continue the process until all of the enchiladas are formed and placed side by side in the skillet. Drizzle the remaining enchilada sauce on top and sprinkle on the remaining cheese.

8. Cover the skillet and cook the enchiladas over medium-low heat until the cheese melts on top and the sauce bubbles throughout, about 10 minutes. Serve with pico de gallo (below) and tortilla chips.

★ Pico de Gallo ★

1 white onion, chopped

5 Roma tomatoes, chopped

4 serrano peppers, chopped

1 bunch cilantro

Juice of 2 limes

Salt to taste

Tortilla chips, for serving

1. In a large bowl, combine the onion, tomatoes, serrano peppers, and cilantro. Drizzle with the lime juice and season with salt. Serve with tortilla chips for dipping.

———————————

Chicken Curry and Roti

SALMAH

Every Guyanese childhood is sprinkled with memories of devouring plate after plate of chicken curry and roti—a dish that represents the Indian influences on our culture. From parties to weddings and every celebration in between, chicken curry and roti will be on the menu, guaranteed. I learned to make this dish by watching my mom, being present, and helping her cook, and it's one of the first meals I prepared on my own. Roti flatbread, of course, is the side dish of choice for any curry, and the most common pairing in all Guyanese cuisine. It took me some time to perfect it, but like making curry, the more you cook it, the better you get! **Serves 6**

1. Season the chicken pieces all over with salt, black pepper, half of the scallions, and 1 teaspoon of the dried thyme. Set aside to marinate while you make the curry.

2. In a large, heavy-bottomed pot, heat the oil over medium heat. Add the cinnamon, cloves, cardamom, and wiri wiri peppers. When the spices begin to sizzle, add the culantro, onion, and remaining scallions and sauté until the onion is pale and softened, about 5 minutes. Add the garlic and sauté until fragrant, 5–7 minutes.

3. In the meantime, bring a kettle of water to a boil.

4. In a small bowl, combine the curry powder, cumin, garam masala, turmeric, remaining 1 teaspoon dried thyme, and salt. Add the spice mixture to the pot and vigorously stir into the sautéed mixture. Toast and bloom the spices just until fragrant, about 3 minutes. Add the tomato and stir.

5. Add ¼ cup boiling water; the dry spices will absorb the water and quickly form a paste. Add a little more boiling water if needed, but let everything sauté and fry together to form a curry paste. Turn the heat down to medium-low and sauté for 20 minutes, adding more boiling water if needed. The onion and tomato will melt into the thick curry paste.

6. When you see the oil slightly separate from the paste, add the chicken and stir to coat the chicken pieces with the paste. Partially cover the pot and cook for 10 minutes.

7. Add the potatoes, then pour in just enough boiling water to cover the chicken and potatoes. Season with salt, black pepper, and thyme. Bring the curry to a boil, then lower the heat to a simmer and cook until the potatoes are soft and the chicken begins to separate from the bone, 25–30 minutes. Remove the cardamom pods before serving. Serve with roti (recipe follows).

1 (3- to 4-pound) whole chicken, skin removed, cut into 10 pieces

Salt and cracked black pepper to taste

1 bunch scallions, chopped, divided

2 teaspoons dried thyme, divided, plus more for seasoning

1 tablespoon vegetable oil

1 cinnamon stick

3 whole cloves

2 cardamom pods, split

4 wiri wiri peppers

3 culantro sprigs, chopped

1 large yellow onion, diced

5 garlic cloves, grated

2 tablespoons curry powder

1 tablespoon ground cumin

1 tablespoon West Indian garam masala

1 tablespoon ground turmeric

1 large tomato, diced

3 large potatoes, quartered

(recipe continues)

★ Roti ★

3 cups all-purpose flour, plus more for dusting

1 teaspoon baking powder

¼ cup vegetable shortening

1¼ cups warm water

Vegetable oil, for greasing and brushing

1. In a large bowl, combine the flour and baking powder. Add the vegetable shortening and press into the dry ingredients. Make a well in the center of the mixture, then slowly stream in the warm water and bring the dough together, squeezing the flour into the water to begin to bring the dough together.

2. Dump the loose dough onto a floured surface and lightly knead, forming a soft dough ball. Be careful not to over-knead. Return the dough ball to the bowl, drizzle with about 1 teaspoon oil, and cover with a damp paper towel. Let rest for 15 minutes.

3. Divide the dough into 6 equal pieces. On a floured surface, roll a piece of dough into a large, thin disk.

4. Brush about 1 tablespoon oil on the disk and sprinkle with flour. Cut a line from the center of the dough disk to the edge and roll the dough to form a cone. Holding the cone up in your hand, tuck the tip into the opening in the center of the cylinder to form a dough ball. Repeat to form the other dough pieces. Cover and let sit for 10 minutes.

5. Preheat a large crepe pan or tawa (traditional cast iron skillet for roti) over medium-high heat.

6. Roll out one of the roti doughs into a large, thin disk 6–8 inches in diameter. Place the roti on the hot skillet or tawa, keeping a close eye as air pockets fill, and cook for 20–30 seconds. Brush with oil and flip, then cook on the other side until brown spots appear, 30 seconds to 1 minute. Place the cooked roti in a paper towel–lined bowl and rest for 10 seconds. Clap the cooked roti between your hands to break the air pockets, then fold into quarters. Repeat to cook the remaining roti.

Kitchri with Stewed Chicken and Mango Pickle

SALMAH

When I think of comfort, my grandmother's kitchri is what comes to mind. Rice and yellow split peas boiled in coconut milk with wilted spinach—these simple ingredients come together in a dish that's like a warm embrace. Chunkay is the Guyanese term for adding spices and garlic cooked in oil to the cooked split peas. Chunkaying infuses the mellow kitchri with flavor and elevates it. Kitchri in our house was always served with stewed chicken, a simple fry in tomato paste, seasoning, onion, and garlic. **Serves 2–3**

Kitchri

2½–3 cups water

½ cup yellow split peas

Salt to taste

1 cup parboiled rice

4 scallions, chopped

1 small yellow onion, diced

2 wiri wiri peppers, seeded and finely chopped

9 garlic cloves, minced, divided

1 (13.5-ounce) can coconut milk

1 cup chopped spinach

1 tablespoon vegetable oil

1 tablespoon mustard seeds

1 tablespoon cumin seeds

Stewed chicken

1 pound boneless, skinless chicken thighs, cut into strips

Salt and ground black pepper to taste

3 culantro sprigs, chopped

1 tablespoon dried thyme, plus more for seasoning

2 tablespoons vegetable oil

1 small yellow onion, diced

3 garlic cloves, minced

1 wiri wiri pepper, seeded and finely chopped

2 Roma tomatoes

¼ cup tomato paste

2 tablespoons paprika

1 teaspoon brown sugar

½ cup water

1. To make the kitchri, in a large, heavy-bottomed pot, combine the water and split peas, season with salt, and bring to a soft boil. Cook for 10 minutes until the peas are a tad soft, then add the rice, scallions, onion, wiri wiri peppers, and half the garlic. Season with salt. Stir, cover the pan, and let simmer for 8 minutes. Pour in the coconut milk and simmer uncovered, stirring occasionally, for 5–8 minutes. Cover again and simmer until the kitchri thickens, the rice and peas are soft, and most of the liquid has been absorbed, about 10 more minutes. Stir in the spinach until it wilts.

2. In a small saucepan, heat the oil over medium heat. Add the remaining garlic, mustard seeds, and cumin seeds. Heat until the spices are fragrant and the garlic is golden, about 5 minutes.

3. Uncover the kitchri and, in one swift motion, tip the tempered spice mixture upside down into the pot and quickly cover the pot to engulf kitchri with smoky flavor.

4. To make the chicken, season the chicken strips with salt, black pepper, culantro, and dried thyme.

(recipe continues)

5. Heat the oil in a large skillet over medium heat. Add the onion, garlic, and wiri wiri pepper. Sauté until fragrant, 5–8 minutes. Add the tomatoes, chicken, tomato paste, paprika, and brown sugar. Season with more salt and thyme and cook until golden brown, about 10 minutes. Add the water, turn the heat up to high, and simmer until a thick gravy has formed and the chicken is tender, about 10 minutes.

6. Serve the kitchri and chicken with mango pickle (below).

№ 2 | Mango Pickle

1 green (unripe) mango, peeled and pitted

1 wiri wiri or Scotch bonnet pepper, finely minced

1 garlic clove, finely minced

¼ cup white vinegar

1 tablespoon salt

1 tablespoon ground black pepper

1. Using a box grater, grate the mango into a large bowl.

2. In a small bowl, combine the wiri wiri pepper, garlic, vinegar, salt, and black pepper and mix well.

3. Pour the spicy vinegar mixture over the mango, mix well, and leave to steep for at least 20 minutes before serving.

Chicken and Dumplings with Cucumber and Onion Salad

KHELA

My mom is from the Carolinas, and one of her staple meals is chicken and dumplings with fried corn-bread. It is a family favorite. When we were kids, my brother, sister, and I would request it for each of our birthday dinners. Sometimes I'll make it in a pinch by putting chicken thighs in the pressure cooker instead of doing the long process with a whole chicken—and that's what this quick recipe calls for. (If I'm being really lazy, I'll pick up a rotisserie chicken from the grocery, but don't ever tell my mom that—I might be disowned!) **Serves 6**

(recipe continues)

1½–1¾ pounds boneless, skinless chicken thighs

½ teaspoon poultry seasoning, divided

4 garlic cloves, 2 halved and 2 grated

2 medium onions, 1 thickly sliced and 1 diced

4 celery stalks, 2 sliced into thirds crosswise and 2 diced

8 cups chicken stock

Leaves from 3–5 thyme sprigs

2 cups all-purpose flour, plus more for dusting

½ teaspoon baking powder

2–3 tablespoons vegetable shortening, bacon grease, unsalted butter, or lard

¾ cup buttermilk

2 tablespoons unsalted butter

2 carrots, diced

Salt and ground black pepper to taste

Splash Maggi seasoning (optional)

1 tablespoon cornstarch (optional)

1. Put the rack in the bottom of an Instant Pot. Place half of the chicken thighs on the rack in a single layer and sprinkle with ¼ teaspoon of the poultry seasoning. Layer the halved garlic cloves, sliced onion, and sliced celery on top so that it will leave space between the next layer of chicken. Add the remaining chicken and sprinkle with the remaining ¼ teaspoon poultry seasoning. Pour in 1 cup water. Lock the lid into place and set to sealing. Cook on high pressure for 8 minutes.

2. Meanwhile, pour the stock into a Dutch oven and bring to a simmer over medium-high heat. Add the thyme and half of the grated garlic.

3. To make the dumplings, in a large bowl, combine the flour, baking powder, and shortening with a pastry cutter until the mixture is crumbly. Add the buttermilk a little at a time and mix gently until it is combined. Flour the top a little and then roll out the dough on a floured surface to about ⅛ inch thick. Using a pizza cutter, cut into roughly 1 × 2-inch strips. Drop the dough strips into the simmering stock a few at a time so they don't stick, stirring after each addition. Cook until the dumplings are cooked through, 18–22 minutes.

4. While the dumplings are cooking, in a large skillet, heat the butter over medium heat. Add the diced onion, diced celery, and carrots and sauté for 2 minutes. Add the remaining grated garlic and cook for another minute. Season with salt and pepper. Add the sautéed vegetable mixture to the broth, along with the Maggi seasoning (if using).

5. When the chicken is done, transfer it to a plate to cool slightly, then cut into bite-size pieces. (Discard the remaining contents of the Instant Pot.) When the dumplings are nearly done, add the chicken to the broth. (If the broth isn't thick enough, add a cornstarch slurry to tighten it up; whisk 1 tablespoon cornstarch with 1 tablespoon of the broth in a small bowl, then stir it into the pot. If it is too thick, add a little more stock or milk.)

6. Serve with cucumber and onion salad (recipe on the next page).

★ Cucumber and Onion Salad ★

3–4 tablespoons white balsamic vinegar

2 tablespoons water

1 teaspoon honey

1 English cucumber, thinly sliced

½ medium sweet onion, thinly sliced

2–3 dill sprigs, chopped

Salt and ground black pepper to taste

1. In a medium bowl, whisk together the vinegar, water, and honey. Add
   the cucumber, onion, and dill and toss to coat. Season with salt and
   pepper. Cover and refrigerate until ready to serve.

Meat Mains

Baharat–Spiced Rack of Lamb with Cherry–Tamarind Sauce

BRAD

You can never really go wrong with a rack of lamb. It's one of those foods that, when done correctly, is a guaranteed showstopper. With something so beautiful and tasty as lamb, I believe less is more when it comes to seasoning, letting the lamb flavor shine. I gently spice the rack of lamb with baharat, garlic, and some fresh rosemary to simply enhance the already amazing flavors this cut of meat yields. It pairs perfectly with my Syrian-inspired cherry-tamarind sauce. **Serves 6**

1. Preheat the oven to 450 degrees F.

2. Place the racks of lamb meat side up in a large roasting pan. Season them all over with the baharat, garlic, salt, pepper, rosemary, and olive oil. Roast for 25 minutes, or until they reach 140 degrees F (for medium-rare).

3. Meanwhile, make the sauce. In a small saucepan, combine the tamarind, the cherries, liquid from the canned cherries, lemon juice, sugar, and allspice and bring to a boil over medium-high heat. Cover, lower the temperature, and let the sauce simmer until reduced and thickened, about 20 minutes. Keep warm until ready to serve.

4. Carve the racks of lamb between the bones. Serve with the cherry-tamarind sauce and garnish with fresh dill.

Lamb

3 racks of lamb, frenched (3 bones per person)

2 tablespoons baharat spice blend

2 heads garlic, cloves separated, peeled, and minced

Kosher salt and ground black pepper to taste

Chopped fresh rosemary to taste

Olive oil, for drizzling

Fresh dill, for garnish

Cherry-tamarind sauce

1 (7-ounce) jar tamarind paste

1 (15-ounce) can sweet cherries, drained and liquid reserved

Juice of 3 lemons

Sugar to taste

Ground allspice to taste

Geera Lamb Chops with Hummus

Lamb chops are rated as a fancy dish in my book—and this dish is an ode to my journey as a home cook! When I was growing up, lamb was prepared and enjoyed as a curry in our household. After getting married and purchasing my first rack of lamb, I seasoned it the best way I knew how: with a dry rub of garam masala, curry powder, and roasted geera (cumin seeds), bound together with grated garlic and a touch of olive oil. Blitzing chickpeas and other ingredients in the food processor makes an easy hummus to offset the gaminess of the lamb chops. **Serves 3–4**

SALMAH

1. Preheat the oven to 350 degrees F. Place a rimmed baking sheet in the oven as it preheats.

2. In a small skillet, toast the cumin and coriander seeds over medium heat until fragrant, about 3 minutes. Transfer the toasted seeds to a small bowl and add the garam masala, curry powder, garlic, thyme, and pomegranate molasses. Mix well to create a semi-dry rub.

3. Pat the rack of lamb dry with paper towels. Liberally rub the spice mixture into the lamb on all sides and season with salt and pepper. Generously drizzle on olive oil to coat.

4. Heat a large skillet on the stovetop over high heat. Sear the rack of lamb on all sides to form a crust and seal in the juices, about 8 minutes. Carefully place the rack of lamb on the hot baking sheet in the oven and roast for 15–20 minutes, until the juices run clear and the internal temperature is 140 degrees F.

5. Remove the baking sheet from the oven, cover tightly with aluminum foil, and set aside to allow the meat to continue to cook for 10 minutes. Carve the rack between the bones. Serve the lamb chops with hummus (below).

3 tablespoons cumin seeds
1 tablespoon coriander seeds
1 teaspoon garam masala
1 teaspoon curry powder
5 garlic cloves, grated
Dried thyme to taste
1 tablespoon pomegranate molasses
1 rack of lamb (6–8 bones)
Salt and cracked black pepper to taste
Olive oil, for drizzling

★ Hummus ★

1 (16-ounce) can chickpeas, drained and rinsed
2 garlic cloves, peeled
⅓ cup olive oil
½ cup tahini
Juice of 2 lemons
2 teaspoons sumac
1 teaspoon salt
1 teaspoon freshly cracked black pepper
10 ice cubes (about ½ cup)

1. In a food processor, combine the chickpeas, garlic, olive oil, tahini, lemon juice, sumac, salt, and pepper. Puree the mixture until it forms a grainy paste.

2. Slowly add the ice cubes, while continuing to puree the hummus, until it slowly blends into a smooth paste. Transfer to a bowl and chill until ready to use.

Lamb Kabobs with Yogurt Sauce and Grilled Veggies

Back when I was in college, I loved going to Kabob Night with the Persian Club. The food was always amazing, the music was great, and the belly dancers were so talented. The entire experience was fantastic, but the highlight for me was always the lamb kabobs. I didn't grow up eating lamb, so it was a new and quite welcome taste. After years of going to metro Atlanta Persian restaurants and peppering all of my Persian friends for tips on how to make lamb kabobs at home, I finally came up with a recipe that I feel comfortable serving to others. **Serves 8**

1. Put the ground lamb in a large bowl and set aside.

2. Put the onion in a food processor and process to a pulp. Empty the onion pulp into a strainer set over the sink or a bowl and press with the back of a spoon to release the liquid from the onion. Once you have removed as much liquid as you can from the onion pulp, add the pulp to the bowl with the lamb (discard the onion liquid).

3. Add the garlic, turmeric, paprika, salt, pepper, and sumac to the bowl with the lamb. Wearing gloves if you wish (the turmeric stains!), massage the onion, garlic, and spices into the lamb until everything is evenly distributed.

4. Take a large handful of the lamb mixture and form it into a log shape around a flat kabob skewer. Repeat this process until all the ground lamb has been used; you should get about 8 kabobs.

5. Brush a cast iron grill pan with the olive oil and heat over medium-high heat. Add as many kabobs as you can fit while leaving about ½ inch in between. Cook, turning to brown the kabobs on all sides, until the meat has reached an internal temperature of at least 160 degrees F. Take care not to overcook, or the kabobs will turn out dry. Transfer to a platter. Wipe the grill pan with paper towels.

6. Lightly brush the red onions, tomatoes, and zucchinis with olive oil and season lightly with salt and pepper.

7. Brush the grill pan with oil and add the vegetables. Grill to the desired doneness, flipping to get char marks on both sides. Transfer to a platter.

8. Serve the kabobs and vegetables with yogurt sauce (below).

Kabobs

2 pounds ground lamb

1 medium white onion, quartered

5 garlic cloves, minced

1 tablespoon ground turmeric

1 teaspoon smoked paprika

1½ teaspoons kosher salt

1 teaspoon ground black pepper

2 tablespoons sumac

1 tablespoon extra-virgin olive oil

Grilled vegetables

2 medium red onions, thickly sliced

6–8 tomatoes, halved

2–3 zucchinis, thickly sliced

Olive oil, for brushing

Salt and ground black pepper to taste

★ Yogurt Sauce ★

1 cup plain whole-milk yogurt

1 cup finely diced Persian or English cucumber

¼ teaspoon lemon juice

2 teaspoons chopped fresh dill

Salt and ground black pepper to taste

1. In a small bowl, mix the yogurt, cucumber, lemon juice, and dill together. Season with salt and pepper.

Bacon–Wrapped Meatloaf with Mushroom Gravy and Mashed Potatoes

KHELA

My husband told me he hated meatloaf because his childhood babysitter had served a terrible one every Thursday. I had a hankering and made one anyway. After I persuaded him to just try it, he proclaimed, "This is my new favorite dish. Why haven't you made it before?" My meatloaf is a little different, with balsamic and tomato paste for the glaze instead of ketchup, and we can't forget the bacon. The mashed potatoes are quick and easy in the pressure cooker and extra special with cheese . . . who doesn't love cheese?! Meatloaf, mashers, and gravy epitomize comfort food. It is like a hug on a plate. **Serves 6**

Meatloaf

1½ pounds ground chuck or sirloin (80% lean)

1½ pounds ground pork

3 large eggs, lightly beaten

1½ cups panko bread crumbs

⅓–½ cup finely chopped fresh chives

2 garlic cloves, minced

3 tablespoons heavy cream

½ cup dry red wine

1 tablespoon chopped fresh thyme

Salt and ground black pepper to taste

Pinch red pepper flakes

2 pounds sliced bacon

Maldon salt, to finish

Glaze

½ cup balsamic glaze

¼ cup tomato paste

1½ teaspoons Italian seasoning

Salt and ground black pepper to taste

Pinch red pepper flakes

1. Preheat the oven to 400 degrees F. Line a rimmed baking sheet with parchment paper.

2. In a large bowl, combine the ground meats, eggs, panko, chives, garlic, cream, wine, thyme, salt, black pepper, and red pepper flakes. Be careful not to overmix. Transfer the meat mixture to the prepared baking sheet and form into 2 equal-size loaves.

3. In a small bowl, mix all the glaze ingredients together. Brush about one-quarter of the glaze on the tops of the loaves.

4. Layer the bacon slices over the loaves, making sure that each slice overlaps and tucks under the meat. Brush the loaves with the remaining glaze until each is covered.

5. Bake for 40–50 minutes, until the internal temperature is at least 155 degrees F. Sprinkle with some Maldon salt. Let the loaves rest before slicing. Serve with mushroom gravy and cmashed potatoes (recipes follow).

★ Mushroom Gravy ★

2 tablespoons vegetable oil

16–24 ounces cremini mushrooms, sliced

2 garlic cloves, grated

2 tablespoons unsalted butter

2 tablespoons all-purpose flour

2–2½ cups beef stock

2 teaspoons Worcestershire sauce

1 teaspoon fish sauce (optional)

1. Heat the oil in a large skillet over medium-high heat. Add the mushrooms and sauté until lightly browned, about 5 minutes. When they are almost done, turn the heat down to medium-low, add the garlic, and cook for a minute or two. Transfer the mushrooms to a plate.

2. Add the butter and flour to the pan and whisk to make a smooth roux. Slowly stir in the beef stock, Worcestershire, and fish sauce (if using), a little at a time. Cook until it thickens into a gravy consistency, about 10 minutes. When it's at the consistency you want, return the mushrooms to the pan. You can add some of the jus from the meatloaf when it finishes for extra flavor.

★ Mashed Potatoes ★

3 pounds Yukon Gold potatoes, quartered

12 tablespoons (1½ sticks) unsalted butter, or more if you like

1 (16-ounce) container mascarpone cheese

¼–½ cup heavy cream

1–2 sprinkles freshly grated nutmeg

Salt and ground black pepper to taste

2–3 fresh chives, finely chopped (optional)

1. Place a steamer basket in the Instant Pot, add the potatoes, and pour in 1 cup water. Lock the lid into place and set to sealing. Cook on high pressure for 11 minutes. Release the pressure naturally for 10 minutes, then manually release the remaining pressure, press "cancel," and remove the lid. (Alternatively, put the potatoes in a large saucepan and cover with 1–2 inches salted water. Bring to a boil and cook until the potatoes are fork-tender, about 20 minutes.)

2. Drain the potatoes when done and return them to the Instant Pot or saucepan. Add the butter, mascarpone, ¼ cup cream, and nutmeg and begin to mash. Add more cream as needed to achieve the desired consistency. Season with salt and pepper and top with chives, if you like.

Beef and Lamb Semolina Meatballs in Spicy Red Sauce

BRAD

This is one of my go-to dishes when cooking for a large group. Ground meat is generally an economical option and a little can go a long way. And it's delicious, so it's a win-win. Inspired by my Grandma Marcia's Thanksgiving meatballs, my dairy-free beef and lamb meatballs are seasoned with spices and fresh herbs that ensure they're packed with flavor but also extremely light and airy. Serve these with your favorite garlic bread. **Serves 12**

Meatballs

1 pound ground lamb

1 pound ground beef

3 large eggs, beaten

1 bunch parsley, finely chopped

1 bunch cilantro, finely chopped

1 bunch dill, finely chopped

1 tablespoon baharat spice

Kosher salt and ground black pepper to taste

1 teaspoon ground cinnamon

1 teaspoon chicken consommé powder

1½ tablespoons tomato paste

½ cup vegetable oil

½ cup semolina

5 garlic cloves, minced

Spicy red sauce

Vegetable oil, for coating

1 onion, chopped

3 garlic cloves, minced

1 (6-ounce) can tomato paste

1½ tablespoons hot paprika

1 tablespoon baharat spice

1½ teaspoons chicken consommé powder

1½ teaspoons ground cumin

3 dried chiles

Kosher salt and ground black pepper to taste

1. Preheat the broiler. Grease a rimmed baking sheet.

2. In a large bowl, combine all of the meatball ingredients and mash together until evenly combined and sticky. Form the mixture into balls of the desired size, making sure they are all the same size for even cooking.

3. Place the meatballs on the prepared baking sheet and broil until browned but not fully cooked, turning occasionally to brown on all sides, 8–10 minutes. Remove the baking sheet from the oven and set aside. Turn the oven to 325 degrees F.

4. Meanwhile, make the sauce. Coat the bottom of a large cast iron skillet with oil and heat over medium-high heat. Add the onion and garlic and sauté until the onion is translucent, about 5 minutes. Add the remaining ingredients, stir, and bring the mixture to a boil. Turn the heat down and simmer until the meatballs are ready.

5. Add the meatballs to the sauce and bring the mixture back to a simmer. Carefully place the skillet in the oven and bake for 30 minutes, or until the meatballs are cooked through.

6. Remove the pan from the oven and let rest for 5 minutes before serving.

Dry–Aged Rib Steak with Fried Potato Wedges and String Beans

BRAD

Rib steak is my ideal date-night meal, because what says "I love you" more than a big hunk of meat? When cooking large cuts of beef, especially ones that are so simply prepared, quality is key. Always get the best cut you can afford. It's not all about price; look for cuts that are dry-aged, prime-grade, and nicely marbled. Don't be shy to have a conversation with your butcher, and if you are presented with a cut that doesn't fit your vision, ask if there is something else available. **Serves 6**

Steaks

6 prime-grade, well-marbled, dry-aged bone-in steaks (1½–2 inches thick)

Kosher salt and ground black pepper to taste

Vegetable oil, for coating

3 tablespoons nondairy butter

3–4 garlic cloves, minced

1 small bunch thyme, leaves chopped

1 small bunch rosemary, leaves chopped

Potato wedges

Kosher salt and ground black pepper to taste

2 tablespoons white vinegar

4 pounds russet potatoes, cut into wedges

1 tablespoon paprika

¾ cup cornstarch

¼ cup baking powder

Vegetable oil, for frying

2 bunches parsley, chopped

1 small bunch rosemary, leaves chopped

String beans

Vegetable oil, for coating

3 shallots, sliced

5 garlic cloves, minced

2 pounds string beans

¼ cup water

Kosher salt and ground black pepper to taste

---

1. Preheat the oven to 200 degrees F. Set a wire rack over a rimmed baking sheet.

2. Pat the steaks dry and season generously with salt and pepper. Place the steaks on the rack and bake until the internal temperature is 5 degrees less than your desired doneness (medium rare is 130–140 degrees F; medium is 140–150 degrees F). Remove from the oven and let rest while you make the potatoes and string beans. The steak will continue to cook as it rests.

3. Bring a large pot of salted water to a boil. Add the vinegar and potatoes and boil until fork-tender, about 15 minutes. Drain the potatoes and pat dry with paper towels.

4. In a large bowl, combine the paprika, cornstarch, and baking powder. Coat the potatoes with the cornstarch mixture.

5. Pour ½ cup oil into another large, heavy pot and heat over medium-high heat to 375 degrees F. Working in batches if necessary, add the potato wedges to the hot oil and fry until crispy, about 3 minutes. Transfer to paper towels. Season with salt and chopped parsley and rosemary.

(recipe continues)

6. To make the string beans, coat the bottom of a sauté pan with oil and heat over medium heat. Add the shallots and garlic and cook until softened, 8–10 minutes. Add the string beans and water and season with salt and pepper. Cover and simmer for 5 minutes. Uncover and continue to cook until the water evaporates and the beans are cooked through, about 5 minutes.

7. Coat the bottom of a large cast iron skillet or grill pan with oil and heat over medium-high heat until you see it just starting to smoke. Add the steaks and sear until nicely browned, about 90 seconds per side. In the last minute of cooking, add the nondairy butter, garlic, thyme, and rosemary and constantly baste the steaks with the butter.

8. Serve the steaks with the potato wedges and string beans.

Hawaiian Plate Lunch

Laulau, Rice, Mac Salad, Lomi Salmon, and Shoyu Poke

The Hawaiian plate is a go-to meal for Hawaiians and tourists alike. It's the ultimate mixed plate of all things Hawai'i served up to go and packed with flavor. You can find these at food trucks and mom-and-pop shops, or even better, make it from scratch at home. You won't be disappointed. **Serves 6**

Hawaiian-style macaroni salad

Salt and ground black pepper to taste

Vegetable oil, for pasta water

8 ounces elbow macaroni

2 tablespoons apple cider vinegar

1 cup mayonnaise

½ cup milk

1 tablespoon sugar

1 carrot, grated

2 tablespoons finely chopped onion

Laulau

1 pound boneless beef short ribs

1 pound pork butt, cut into 1-inch cubes

1 tablespoon Hawaiian salt

1 tablespoon grated fresh ginger

1 tablespoon beef base (such as Better Than Bouillon)

1 cup water

1 pound lū'au (taro) leaves

12 fresh ti leaves

Rice

3 cups medium-grain white rice, such as Calrose

3 cups water

Lomi salmon

8 ounces salmon, finely chopped

1 bunch scallions, finely chopped

1 small sweet Maui onion, finely chopped

2 medium tomatoes, finely chopped

Shoyu poke

1 pound sashimi-grade ahi tuna, cut into ½- to ¾-inch cubes

¼ cup thinly sliced scallions

¼ cup thinly sliced sweet Maui onion

2 tablespoons shoyu or soy sauce

1 teaspoon toasted sesame oil

---

1. To make the Hawaiian-style macaroni salad, bring a large pot of water to a rolling boil. Add salt and a splash of oil to the water. Add the macaroni and cook according to the package directions to just past the al dente stage. Drain the noodles and rinse with water. Transfer the noodles to a medium bowl and toss with the vinegar.

2. In a small bowl, whisk together the mayonnaise, milk, sugar, salt, and pepper. Add the mayonnaise mixture to the noodles and stir to combine. Add the carrot and onion and stir until well combined. Cover and refrigerate for 4 hours, or overnight.

3. To make the laulau, select sauté mode on an Instant Pot. Put the beef and pork in the pot and cook until browned on all sides, 10–15 minutes. Add the Hawaiian salt, ginger, beef base, and water. Press "cancel." Lock the lid into place and set to sealing. Cook on high pressure for 25 minutes. Allow natural pressure release for 10 minutes, then quick release.

(recipe continues)

4. While the meat is cooking, bring a large pot of water to a boil. Add the lū'au leaves and boil until soft, 10–15 minutes. Drain the cooked lū'au leaves. Add a ladle of the broth from the Instant Pot to the lū'au leaves.

5. Lay two ti leaves in a cross pattern on a cutting board. Add a heaping tablespoon of the lū'au leaves to the center of the ti leaves. Then add some of the beef and pork, and top with another heaping tablespoon of the cooked lū'au leaves. Bring the ends of the ti leaves together and tie with butcher's twine.

6. To make the rice, rinse the rice under cool running water until the water runs clear. Put the rice and water in a rice cooker and set to cook.

7. To make the lomi salmon, combine the salmon, scallions, onion, and tomatoes in a medium bowl and toss to combine. Add a few ice cubes to the bowl, cover, and refrigerate until ready to serve. The salmon can be quite salty, so the ice cubes will help dilute it slightly as they melt.

8. Just before serving, make the shoyu poke. In a medium bowl, combine the ahi, scallions, onion, shoyu, and sesame oil and stir gently to combine.

9. To serve, place a laulau bundle on each plate. Add a scoop each of rice, macaroni salad, lomi salmon, and poke. Serve immediately.

Kalbi Beef Tenderloin with Bok Choy and Ube Mash

GRAHAM

Living on the beautiful islands of Hawai'i has exposed me to so many exciting flavors and ingredients. Hawai'i is a true melting pot, heavily influenced by China, Japan, Korea, and the Philippines. This recipe is a play on the classic Korean barbecued beef, but has been switched up with beef tenderloin in place of short ribs. The ube (Okinawan sweet potato) adds a richness and slightly sweet flavor, which is much more exciting than a standard mashed potato. The bok choy ties everything together. **Serves 4**

1. In a blender, combine the onion, brown sugar, soy sauce, mirin, water, garlic, sesame oil, and sriracha and blend for 1–2 minutes at high speed until thoroughly combined.

2. Place the beef tenderloin filets in a large resealable plastic bag and pour in the marinade. Squeeze the excess air out of the bag and seal, then press to distribute the marinade over the steaks. Place the bag in a shallow dish and refrigerate for at least 6 hours, preferably overnight, turning the bag over occasionally to ensure that the marinade is penetrating the steaks evenly.

3. Preheat a grill to medium-high heat. Transfer the steaks to a plate. Pat both sides of the steaks dry with a paper towel. Grill the steaks until they register an internal temperature of 130 degrees F, 5–7 minutes per side. The steaks will continue to cook as they rest. Rest the steaks in a warm location for 10–15 minutes. Turn the grill down to medium.

4. Meanwhile, put the sweet potatoes in a medium saucepan and cover with cold water. Bring the water to a boil, then reduce to a vigorous simmer. Cook the sweet potatoes until fully tender, 15–20 minutes. Drain the sweet potatoes, then return them to the pot. Add the butter and mash with a potato masher to incorporate the butter. Add the warm heavy cream and continue to mash until the sweet potatoes are smooth but still fluffy. Season with salt and pepper to taste.

5. Slice the bok choy lengthwise and place in a large bowl. Drizzle with olive oil, season with salt and pepper, and toss to combine. Place the bok choy halves cut side down on the grill and grill for a few minutes on each side, until they are just tender. Remove from the heat and re-season if necessary.

6. To plate, place the sweet potato mash in the center of each plate and arrange the grilled bok choy alongside. Place a beef tenderloin steak alongside the bok choy and garnish with scallions.

1 cup roughly chopped yellow onion

¾ cup brown sugar

¾ cup soy sauce

¼ cup mirin

¼ cup water

10 garlic cloves, peeled

2 tablespoons toasted sesame oil

1 tablespoon sriracha

4 (8-ounce) beef tenderloin filets

2 pounds Okinawan sweet potatoes, peeled and cut into large chunks

8 tablespoons (1 stick) unsalted butter, cut into chunks

1 cup heavy cream, warmed

Salt and ground black pepper to taste

1½ pounds bok choy

Olive oil, for drizzling

Sliced scallions, for garnish

Pepper Steak

SALMAH

I follow a halal diet, but there are few halal Asian restaurants in my area. Once I learned how to make my own pepper steak, it quickly became a family favorite. This delicious meal is composed of thinly sliced flank steak, fried with sweet peppers and onions, coated in a sweet and spicy sauce, and served over a bed of rice. Prepping the ingredients takes more time than actually cooking the dish; once you have everything ready, you're a quick stir-fry away from dinner, making it a great way to end a hectic day. **Serves 3–4**

¼ cup soy sauce

¼ cup oyster sauce

5 garlic cloves, grated

1-inch piece ginger, grated

1½ teaspoons sugar

2 tablespoons cornstarch

2 pounds flank steak, thinly sliced against the grain

4 tablespoons vegetable oil, divided

Salt and ground black pepper to taste

1 red bell pepper, seeded and sliced

1 green bell pepper, seeded and sliced

3 dried red chiles

1 large onion, sliced

Sesame seeds, for garnish

Sliced scallions, for garnish

Cooked white rice, to serve

1. In a small bowl, whisk together the soy sauce, oyster sauce, garlic, ginger, and sugar. Add the cornstarch and whisk until it is dissolved. Set aside. Season the meat with salt and pepper.

2. In a large skillet, heat 2 tablespoons of the oil over high heat. Add the beef and stir-fry just until it is seared to a nice brown and no longer pink, about 8 minutes. Transfer to a plate.

3. Wipe out the skillet and add the remaining 2 tablespoons oil; heat over medium-high heat. Add the bell peppers, chiles, and onion and sauté until softened, about 5 minutes.

4. Return the beef to the pan. Re-whisk the reserved sauce and pour it over the beef and vegetables. Cook, stirring, until the sauce has slightly thickened, 7–10 minutes. Transfer to a serving dish. Sprinkle with sesame seeds and scallions and serve with rice.

Picanha Steak and Sugar Snaps with Bacon–Sour Cream Potato Salad

TIFFANY

Everyone needs a great steak recipe that doesn't break the bank. My son is always in the mood for a steak, and if he could have steak as a midweek meal it would instantly put a smile on his face. Picanha, also known as coulotte or top sirloin cap, is one of my favorite cuts of beef because it's affordable and simply delicious. When shopping for this cut, make sure to choose a piece with a fat cap. It will allow the meat to remain juicy and tender. This cut is best served medium-rare or medium, and allowing it to rest is crucial! **Serves 4**

1. Score the fat side of the steak, being careful not to cut into the meat. Cut with the grain into two or three large pieces. Season all over with the salt.

2. Heat the grapeseed oil in a large cast iron skillet or heavy-bottomed sauté pan over medium heat. Place the steak pieces, fat side down, in the pan, along with the garlic cloves. Cook for 4 minutes, then add the thyme, butter, and black pepper. Flip the steak pieces and continue to cook, basting with the melted butter, until brown all over, 1–2 minutes per side. Transfer to a plate and allow to rest for 5–10 minutes before carving.

3. Meanwhile, heat the olive oil in a medium sauté pan over medium heat. Add the sugar snap peas and season with salt and pepper. Add the water and cover the pan. Cook until the peas are crisp-tender and the water has evaporated. Add the lemon zest and adjust the seasoning if need be.

4. Slice the beef against the grain and serve with the sugar snaps and bacon–sour cream potato salad (recipe follows).

1 (1½- to 2-pound) picanha steak with fat cap, at room temperature

2 tablespoons kosher salt, plus more to taste

1 tablespoon grapeseed oil or other high–smoke point oil

2 garlic cloves, unpeeled

2 thyme sprigs

1 tablespoon unsalted butter

Cracked black pepper to taste

1 teaspoon olive oil

8 ounces sugar snap peas, cut in half on the diagonal

2 tablespoons water

Grated zest of ¼ lemon

(recipe continues)

★ Bacon–Sour Cream Potato Salad ★

1 pound Yukon Gold potatoes, scrubbed and cut into 1-inch pieces

1 teaspoon kosher salt, plus more for cooking the potatoes

2 tablespoons apple cider vinegar

½ cup mayonnaise

¼ cup sour cream

1 tablespoon whole-grain mustard

1 teaspoon ground black pepper

½ teaspoon smoked paprika, plus more for garnish

5–6 slices bacon, cooked and crumbled

2 celery stalks, finely diced

¼ cup finely diced red onion

2 scallions, thinly sliced

2 tablespoons chopped fresh dill

1. Put the potatoes in a large pot and cover with water. Add salt and bring to a boil over high heat. Reduce the heat to medium and cook until the potatoes are fork-tender, about 15 minutes. Using a slotted spoon, transfer the potatoes to a large bowl. Sprinkle the hot potatoes with the vinegar and toss to coat.

2. In a small bowl, combine the mayonnaise, sour cream, mustard, salt, pepper, and smoked paprika and mix well.

3. Add the bacon, celery, onion, and scallions to the potatoes. Add the dressing to the potatoes and toss to combine. Sprinkle with a little extra paprika and the dill.

Bison Short Ribs with Mashed Potatoes and Huckleberry Wojapi

MARIA

There is nothing more Coeur d'Alene than bison and huckleberries. Every summer, I pick berries with my mom and aunties in the mountains of Idaho. I love this wojapi (berry sauce) because it builds on the rich base of browned butter, which complements the sweetness of the berries. This dish is a favorite that can go from simple weeknight dinner to an elevated presentation depending on how you want to plate it. **Serves 6**

1. Using sauté mode on an Instant Pot, melt the butter. Season the ribs with a sprinkling of salt. Add the ribs to the pot and sear until nicely browned on all sides, 10–15 minutes. Work in batches if necessary so as not to crowd. Transfer the short ribs to a plate as they are browned.

2. Add the onion to the pot and cook until translucent and soft, about 2 minutes, then press "cancel." Return the ribs to the pot. Lock the lid into place and set to sealing. Cook on high pressure for 1 hour. Release the pressure manually, press "cancel," and remove the lid. Let the ribs rest while finishing the other components.

3. To make the mashed potatoes, bring a medium saucepan of water to a boil over high heat. Add the potatoes and simmer until tender when tested with a fork, about 20 minutes. Drain the potatoes, then return them to the pot. Add the butter, sour cream, and a pinch of salt. Mash the potatoes with a potato masher until smooth and creamy. Taste and adjust the salt if needed.

4. To make the wojapi, put the huckleberries in a small saucepan and cook over medium heat until they start to burst and liquefy, about 10–15 minutes. Add the maple syrup and simmer for 5 minutes, then add the cornstarch and stir to incorporate evenly. Continue to cook until the sauce thickens slightly, about 10 minutes. Remove from heat and set aside until ready to serve.

5. Serve the short ribs over the mashed potatoes, with the huckleberry sauce on the side.

Bison short ribs

4 tablespoons (½ stick) unsalted butter

8 bison short ribs

Salt to taste

1 yellow onion, chopped

Mashed potatoes

2 cups peeled and diced russet potatoes (about 2 potatoes)

4 tablespoons (½ stick) unsalted butter

½ cup sour cream

Salt to taste

Huckleberry wojapi

1 cup huckleberries

2 tablespoons maple syrup

1 teaspoon cornstarch

Mafrum and Salatim

Meat-Stuffed Vegetables with Salads and Sides

BRAD

The crown jewel of Libyan Jewish cuisine, mafrum is a meat-stuffed vegetable that is fried and then braised until soft. The most traditional mafrum is made with potato, but my favorite is eggplant. This dish is a labor of love and a guaranteed mess in the kitchen, but so worth it. My family would generally enjoy mafrum during the holidays, and whenever I visit my aunts in Israel, they always make it special for me.

Some of the best parts of this dish are the salatim, salads, to accompany it. Matbucha is a Moroccan tomato and pepper salad. Then there's a creamy corn salad, a cucumber salad, and always some hot peppers. On *The Great American Recipe*, I also added my Tershi with Harissa (page 15) to this feast. **Serves 9**

Mafrum

3 eggplants

1 pound ground lamb

1 pound ground beef

3 onions, chopped

1 potato, peeled and grated

1 large bunch parsley

1 large bunch cilantro

8 large eggs, divided

1½ tablespoons baharat

1½ teaspoons ras el hanout

1½ teaspoons chicken consommé powder

1½ teaspoons hot paprika

1½ teaspoons sweet paprika

1½ teaspoons ground cinnamon

1 tablespoon salt

Vegetable oil

2 cups all-purpose flour

1 (6-ounce) can tomato paste

½–1 cup water, if needed

Braising sauce

½ cup chopped onion

1 celery stalk, chopped

1 carrot, chopped

1 small potato, diced

1 small bunch parsley

1 tablespoon baharat

1½ teaspoons chicken consommé powder

1 teaspoon ground cinnamon

1 teaspoon ras el hanout

½ teaspoon ground black pepper

1 cup water

2 tablespoons tomato paste

To serve

Tershi with Harissa (page 15)

Cooked couscous (page 152)

Toasted pine nuts, for garnish

Chopped parsley, for garnish

Israeli spicy peppers, for garnish

---

1. Cut off the ends of each eggplant and then slice each eggplant into 1½ inch thick slices. Cut a slit into each piece of eggplant (don't cut all the way through) to make a sort of eggplant "sandwich bun." You should have 9 eggplant pieces.

2. In a large bowl, combine the meat, onions, potato, herbs, 4 of the eggs, and the seasonings. Stuff the eggplants with the meat mixture.

3. In a large skillet, heat the oil over medium-high heat.

(recipe continues)

4. Put the flour in a shallow dish. In another shallow dish, whisk together the remaining 4 eggs and the tomato paste. Add ½ cup water and mix well. The tomato paste mixture should have the consistency of a thick tomato soup. If it is too thick, thin it out with more water.

5. Dip each mafrum into the tomato paste mixture and then the flour mixture. Add to the hot oil and fry until nicely browned, about 2 minutes per side. Transfer to a plate lined with paper towels.

6. To make the braising sauce, in a large Dutch oven, combine the onion, celery, carrot, potato, and parsley. Place the fried mafrum on top. Add the baharat, consommé powder, cinnamon, ras el hanout, black pepper, water, and tomato paste. Cover and cook over medium heat for about 2 hours, until the sauce thickens and the flavors develop. While the mafrum braises, make the salatim.

7. Serve the mafrum over the cooked couscous and garnish with pine nuts and parsley. Serve the salatim on the side.

★ Matbucha ★

1–2 tablespoons olive oil

3 jalapeño peppers, chopped

2 long hot peppers, chopped

1 head garlic, cloves separated, peeled, and thinly sliced

1 (28-ounce) can whole peeled San Marzano tomatoes

2 tablespoons sweet paprika

2 tablespoons hot paprika

Kosher salt to taste

Cayenne pepper to taste (optional)

1. Heat the oil in a medium skillet over medium heat. Add the peppers and garlic and sauté until soft, about 5 minutes. Add the tomatoes with their juices, reduce the heat, and simmer until thick, about 1 hour. Season with the paprika, salt, and cayenne (if using).

★ Cucumber salad ★

6 seedless cucumbers, thinly sliced

1 large bunch dill, chopped

¼ cup white vinegar

1½ teaspoons salt

½ teaspoon ground black pepper

1. In a large bowl, combine all the ingredients and toss together.

★ Corn salad ★

3 (15-ounce) cans corn, drained

1 (19-ounce) can Israeli pickles, drained and diced small

1 cup mayonnaise

1 large bunch dill, chopped

1½ teaspoons kosher salt

½ teaspoon ground black pepper

3–4 tablespoons white vinegar

1. In a large bowl, combine all the ingredients and toss together.

Baby Back Ribs with Cheesy Corn and Slaw

KHELA

I live in a suburb of Kansas City, where BBQ is serious business. While ribs, cheesy corn, and slaw are standards, my renditions are stamped with the "Khela outside of the box" mark. My BBQ sauce features a little soy sauce and fish sauce . . . as well as banana ketchup instead of the traditional tomatoey stuff. I was first introduced to this magical Filipino ingredient while researching recipes for a region-themed foodie party my friend Angela threw. It plays particularly nice in marinades and glazes. The cheesy corn is a little like mac and cheese, but with corn. It's a staple in KC, made famous by Fiorella's Jack Stack Barbecue restaurant. My take starts with a roux so I can use real cheese instead of the processed stuff, and of course I kick it up with a little heat from jalapeños. Last but not least, there's the vinegary slaw, which gets a little funk from fish sauce to complement the sweetness of the pork and the creamy richness of the corn. **Serves 6–8**

1. Preheat the oven to 400 degrees F.

2. Remove the silverskin from the ribs and cut them between the bones. Pat dry with paper towels, then sprinkle your favorite rub all over the ribs and pat it down with your hands.

3. Put the trivet in the Instant Pot and pour in the broth. Stand the ribs up around the perimeter of the pot, meaty sides out, so they are leaning on each other. Select the sauté mode and cook for 3 minutes so that the pot will heat faster, then press "cancel." Lock the lid into place and set to sealing. Cook at high pressure for 30 minutes. Release the pressure manually, press "cancel," and remove the lid.

4. While the ribs are cooking, in a small bowl, mix together the banana ketchup, dark soy sauce, honey, and fish sauce; set aside. Preheat the broiler on high. Line a rimmed baking sheet with aluminum foil.

5. When the ribs are done, transfer them to the prepared baking sheet. Brush some sauce on both sides of the ribs.

6. Broil for about 2 minutes on each side, just until dark and caramelized. Serve with cheesy corn and slaw (recipes follow).

---

2 racks baby back ribs

¼ cup favorite dry rub (I use Q39 Rib Rub)

2 cups chicken broth

6 tablespoons banana ketchup

2 tablespoons dark soy sauce

2 tablespoons honey

1 teaspoon fish sauce

★ Cheesy Corn ★

1 tablespoon vegetable oil

½ cup diced onion

8 ears corn, kernels removed

1 garlic clove, minced

1 tablespoon seeded
and finely chopped jalapeño

1 tablespoon unsalted butter

1 tablespoon all-purpose flour

¾ cup whole milk

¼ teaspoon freshly ground nutmeg

1½ teaspoons Dijon mustard

⅔ cup shredded sharp cheddar cheese,
divided

½ cup shredded Monterey Jack cheese,
divided

6 bacon slices, cooked and crumbled

2 scallions, chopped

1. In a medium saucepan, heat the oil over medium heat. Add the onion and cook for 2 minutes, then add the corn kernels, garlic, and jalapeño and cook until softened, about 5 minutes. Transfer to a medium bowl.

2. Add the butter and flour to the same pan and cook for 2 minutes over medium-low heat, stirring, to make a roux. Slowly add the milk and simmer for 2–3 minutes to make a béchamel, then add the nutmeg and Dijon.

3. Set aside 2 tablespoons each of the cheddar and Monterey Jack cheeses. Gradually add the rest of the cheese to the pan, stirring it in and letting some of it melt before adding more so it doesn't get grainy. When all the cheese is incorporated, add the corn mixture. Turn the heat down to medium-low and cook for 3–5 minutes, then turn it down to low until ready to serve. (If it isn't thick enough, you can add a little extra cheese.)

4. Stir in most of the bacon, then garnish with the remaining bacon, reserved cheese, and scallions.

★ Slaw ★

1 tablespoon fish sauce

Grated zest of 1 lime

1 tablespoon lime juice

1 teaspoon honey

2 tablespoons olive oil

⅓–½ head green or red cabbage,
finely shredded

1 Granny Smith apple, cored and julienned

1–2 jalapeños, seeded and very thinly sliced

1 celery stalk, thinly sliced

¼–⅓ bunch cilantro, leaves and tender
stems roughly chopped

1 tablespoon chopped fresh mint

Maldon salt, to finish

1. In a large bowl, whisk together the fish sauce, lime zest and juice, honey, and olive oil. Add the cabbage, apple, jalapeño, celery, cilantro, and mint and toss well to coat. Finish with flaky sea salt.

Pork Souvlaki with YiaYia's Tzatziki

TED

Pork souvlaki is a staple in Greek culture. It's not uncommon to have platters of pork souvlaki skewers served up at dinner in a Greek village while enjoying the company of family and friends; the tender marinated pork skewers are perfect for gathering and socializing. So it's no coincidence that these made a regular appearance at the dinner table in my childhood home. My mom, Nancy, would always have something to go along with the pork, and her go-to was tzatziki. Her recipe for this creamy and garlicky side is my favorite and goes perfectly with the marinated pork. **Serves 6**

1. In a medium bowl, whisk together the olive oil, onion (if using), garlic, lemon zest and juice, vinegar, oregano, paprika, dried thyme, salt, and pepper. Transfer the mixture to a resealable plastic bag. Add the pork, seal the bag, and toss to make sure all the pork is covered with the marinade. Refrigerate for at least 4 hours, or overnight.

2. Preheat a grill to medium-high heat. If using wooden skewers, soak them in water.

3. Thread about 6 pieces of pork onto each skewer. Grill the skewers until the pork is cooked through, about 2 minutes each side.

4. Transfer the skewers to a platter and garnish with thyme sprigs, lemon slices, and cubes of feta. Serve with a large spoonful of tzatziki (below).

1 cup Greek olive oil

1 small red onion or shallot, finely chopped (optional)

5 garlic cloves, minced

2 tablespoons grated lemon zest

½ cup fresh lemon juice

2 tablespoons red wine vinegar

2 teaspoons dried Greek oregano

1 teaspoon paprika

1 teaspoon dried thyme

Salt and ground black pepper to taste

3 pounds pork loin, cut into 1½-inch pieces

Thyme sprigs, for garnish

Thin lemon slices, for garnish

6–8 ounces feta cheese, cubed

★ YiaYia's Tzatziki ★

1 English cucumber

3 cups full-fat Greek yogurt

2 tablespoons chopped fresh dill

2 teaspoons chopped fresh mint

2 garlic cloves, minced

1 tablespoon fresh lemon juice

1 tablespoon Greek olive oil

Salt and ground black pepper to taste

1. Grate the cucumber on the large holes of a box grater into a large strainer. Squeeze and press out as much excess liquid as possible. Transfer the cucumber to a bowl. Add the yogurt, dill, mint, garlic, lemon juice, and olive oil and mix thoroughly. Season with salt and pepper. Cover and refrigerate until ready to serve.

Sweet 'n' Sour Spare Ribs with Smashed Purple Sweet Potatoes

RELLE

As a child, I remember my grandmother hauling around this heavy cast iron Dutch oven. When she brought it out I knew she was making her delicious sweet-and-sour spare ribs. Sweet-and-sour spare ribs are a popular Chinese dish in Hawai'i—tender, fall-off-the-bone pork with just a touch of sweet and tang. Add a little pineapple for this Hawaiian-style version and serve it with a delicious and vibrant smashed purple sweet potato. **Serves 8**

Spare ribs

2 tablespoons vegetable oil, divided

3 pounds spare ribs, cut between the bones

½ cup all-purpose flour

1 small onion, sliced

½ cup brown sugar

½ cup rice vinegar

¼ cup pineapple juice

½ cup shoyu or soy sauce

½ cup water

5 garlic cloves, minced

1-inch piece ginger, sliced

2 tablespoons cornstarch

2 tablespoons water

1 fresh pineapple, peeled, cored, and cut into chunks

Sweet potatoes

3 small Okinawan sweet potatoes

½ teaspoon garlic salt

¼ teaspoon ground black pepper

2 tablespoons vegetable oil

1. Heat 1 tablespoon of the oil in a cast iron skillet over high heat. Toss the spare ribs in the flour just to coat. Working in batches, add the spare ribs to the pan and cook until browned on all sides, 10–15 minutes.

2. Using sauté mode on an Instant Pot, heat the remaining 1 tablespoon oil. Add the onion and sauté until translucent, about 5 minutes. Add the spare ribs.

3. In a bowl, combine the brown sugar, vinegar, pineapple juice, shoyu, water, garlic, and ginger and mix well. Pour the mixture into the pot. Press "cancel." Lock the lid in place and set to sealing. Cook on high pressure for 25 minutes. Release the pressure naturally for 10 minutes, then manually release the remaining pressure, press "cancel," and remove the lid.

4. To make the sweet potatoes: Bring a few inches of water to a boil in a pot fitted with a steamer basket. Add the sweet potatoes. Cover, reduce the heat to medium, and steam until the potatoes are fork-tender, 25–30 minutes.

5. Slice the potatoes on the bias about 1 inch thick and place on a cutting board or baking sheet. Using a heavy-bottomed cup or bowl, flatten the potatoes. Season with the garlic salt and pepper.

6. Heat the oil in a large skillet over medium-high heat. Add the potatoes and fry until crispy, 10–15 minutes. Flip and repeat on the other side.

7. In a small bowl, whisk together the cornstarch and water. Add the mixture to the Instant Pot and stir to thicken the sauce. Stir in the pineapple chunks and serve with the smashed purple sweet potatoes.

Fish and Seafood

Chraime with Couscous

BRAD

Chraime is a staple in any Libyan household—a tangy, spicy, garlicky red sauce that's easy enough to make during the week, but delicious enough to have a place on the Shabbat table. Whenever I eat chraime, it brings back fond memories of my Libyan grandmother making food for Shabbat dinner to serve her sixteen children (plus their spouses, children, and grandchildren). It was astonishing.

My family usually serves this fish as an appetizer on Friday evenings, though it most definitely can be made as a main course. Truthfully, it deserves all the limelight! It's best served with couscous, rice, challah, or even matzah on Passover. Really, any vessel that allows you to enjoy every last lick of delicious red sauce is appropriate. **Serves 6–8**

1. Heat 2 tablespoons of the oil in a large skillet over high heat. Season both sides of the salmon with salt, pepper, and a pinch of caraway. Sear the fish for a minute or two on each side, until the skin is golden. Transfer the fish to a plate and wipe the skillet clean.

2. Heat the remaining 3 tablespoons oil in the same skillet over medium heat. Add the garlic, both paprikas, cumin, caraway, and cayenne and cook for 30 seconds, stirring constantly so that the spices don't burn. Add the tomato paste and cook, stirring, for 1 minute. Add the water and lemon juice and bring to a simmer, stirring occasionally. Season with salt and pepper to taste.

3. Return the fish to the skillet, reduce the heat, and bring to a gentle simmer. Cook for about 7 minutes, until the fish is cooked through (145 degrees F).

4. Remove the pan from the heat and allow to cool slightly. Sprinkle a little caraway on the fish. Serve with the pan sauce and couscous (recipe follows), garnished with cilantro, and with lemon wedges for squeezing.

5 tablespoons vegetable oil, divided

3 pounds skin-on or skinless wild salmon fillets, cut into equal-size portions

Kosher salt and ground black pepper to taste

1 tablespoon ground caraway, plus more for sprinkling

1 head garlic, cloves separated, peeled, and crushed

2 tablespoons sweet paprika

2 tablespoons hot paprika

1 tablespoon ground cumin

1 teaspoon cayenne pepper, or to taste

3 tablespoons tomato paste

2 cups water

3 tablespoons freshly squeezed lemon juice, plus lemon wedges for serving

Chopped fresh cilantro, for garnish

(recipe continues)

№ 2 | Couscous

1 (2.2-pound) bag coarse
semolina, such as
Stybel

1 cup vegetable oil

1½ tablespoons kosher
salt

6 cups boiling water

1. In a large microwave-safe bowl, combine the semolina, oil, and salt. Pour the boiling water over the semolina and rake with a fork.

2. Cover the semolina with a clean kitchen towel and microwave for 4 minutes. Rake again, cover again, and microwave for an additional 4 minutes. Rake again, then transfer the couscous to a food processor and pulse to break apart until small and fluffy.

Red Chile Pan–Fried Rocky Mountain Trout with Stuffed Poblanos

ABBE

In the Rocky Mountain region, many love to fish for trout, Rocky Mountain trout being one of the best. My recipe uses many ingredients common to our region, such as blue cornmeal and red chiles. This fun dish is flavored with ancho chile powder and some alder-smoked sea salt to help give it that campfire flavor. And if you love chiles, don't forget the red chile sauce. Perfect over almost anything, this is a staple in my fridge! The stuffed poblanos are a recipe I've made for years and truly are a great accompaniment to this regional dish. **Serves 6**

(recipe continues)

Red chile sauce

2 tablespoons vegetable oil

1 medium onion, minced

3 garlic cloves, minced

½ cup red chile powder, such as ancho or molido

1 teaspoon dried Mexican oregano

1 quart chicken stock or water

1–3 teaspoons honey, divided

¼ teaspoon alder-smoked sea salt

⅓ cup half-and-half

2 tablespoons unsalted butter

Trout

1 tablespoon honey

1 tablespoon vegetable oil

3 garlic cloves, minced

2 teaspoons Dijon mustard

2 tablespoons plus 1 teaspoon red chile powder, such as ancho or molido

½ teaspoon alder-smoked sea salt

6 skin-on trout fillets

6 tablespoons toasted pecans, divided

¼ cup blue cornmeal

½ cup yellow cornmeal

¼ cup panko bread crumbs

1 teaspoon salt

¼ cup olive oil

1. To make the red chile sauce, heat the oil in a medium saucepan over medium heat. Add the onion and garlic and sauté until the onion is limp, about 5 minutes. Stir in the chile powder and oregano and let toast for 1 minute, stirring constantly. Add the stock, ½ cup at a time, while letting the mixture simmer until it reaches the consistency of a sauce. Taste and add honey for the sweetness you prefer, then whisk in the smoked sea salt, half-and-half, and butter.

2. To make the trout, mix together the honey, vegetable oil, garlic, mustard, 1 teaspoon of the red chile powder, and the smoked sea salt in a small bowl. Spread the mustard mixture all over the trout fillets. Let sit at room temperature for 30 minutes. Meanwhile, preheat the oven to 350 degrees F.

3. Combine 4 tablespoons of the pecans, both cornmeals, panko, remaining 2 tablespoons chile powder, and salt in a spice grinder and blend until fine. Transfer to a shallow dish.

4. Heat the olive oil in a large oven-safe skillet over medium heat. Dredge the skin side of each trout fillet in the breading mixture and place in the hot oil, breading side down. Fry until golden, 4–5 minutes. Drizzle the top with some of the oil and place in the oven for about 5 minutes to finish cooking.

5. Serve the trout topped with red chile sauce and the remaining 2 tablespoons toasted pecans, with stuffed poblanos (recipe on the next page) on the side.

№ 2 | Stuffed Poblanos

6 ounces goat cheese or cream cheese

½ cup Stilton cheese with apricots

½ cup grated Parmesan cheese, divided

⅓ cup chopped onion

⅓ cup chopped cilantro

¾ cup roasted corn kernels (thawed if from frozen)

2 garlic cloves, minced

Salt and ground black pepper to taste

2–4 tablespoons heavy cream or half-and-half

6 large poblanos, roasted and peeled

1. Preheat the oven to 400 degrees F.

2. In a small bowl, combine the goat cheese, Stilton, and ¼ cup of the Parmesan and mix using a spoon or an immersion blender if your cheese is too cold. Stir in the onion, cilantro, corn, and garlic. Season with salt and pepper. Mix in the cream until the cheese mixture is the desired consistency for stuffing.

3. Make a slit on one side of each poblano and remove the seeds. Divide the cheese mixture among the peppers. Fold up the sides of each pepper to partially enclose the filling. Sprinkle with the remaining ¼ cup Parmesan.

4. Place the stuffed poblanos in a small baking pan and bake for 15 minutes, or until golden.

Cou–Cou 'n' Flying Fish

LEANNA

Cou-cou and flying fish was a dinner staple when I was a child. After all, it is the national dish of Barbados, and I am a first-generation Bajan-American. Cou-cou is not to be confused with couscous! It's a cornmeal mash, kind of like polenta or grits, that's cooked with okra.

Nowadays flying fish is fairly hard to come by, even in Barbados. I can't believe how expensive it has gotten, rivaled only by oxtails in terms of the price increase over the years. But I pay the price because for me, flying fish is a piece of home. That said, it is difficult to source flying fish outside the Caribbean, so feel free to substitute another flaky, mild white fish, such as flounder, that is readily available. *On The Great American Recipe*, I made it with snapper. **Serves 6**

1. Put the fish in a large bowl. Sprinkle with 1 teaspoon of the salt and squeeze in the lime juice, then gently rub the lime and salt all over both sides of the fish. Cover and refrigerate for 30 minutes.

2. Rinse off the lime and salt and pat the fish dry with a paper towel. Rub a little jerk seasoning in all the crevices on the top of the fish. Set aside.

3. In a medium saucepan, bring 3 cups of the water to a boil over high heat. Add the okra, reduce the heat to low, and bring the water back to a simmer. Cook the okra for 12 minutes. You should see the okra "slime" in the water.

4. Pour the okra and water into a large bowl. Return 1 cup of the okra cooking water to the saucepan, still over low heat. Add the cornmeal and stir, using a wooden spoon or cou-cou stick. Gradually add the remaining okra and okra cooking water, stirring constantly to avoid lumps. Wait for the cornmeal to absorb most of the water before adding more. When all the okra and okra water are mixed into the cornmeal, continue to cook the mixture, stirring occasionally, until it starts to puff, about 20 minutes. Cover and keep warm while you fry the fish.

5. Lightly coat the fish in flour. Heat the oil in a large skillet over medium heat.

6. While the oil is heating up, make the gravy. Combine the onion, oregano, thyme, and remaining 1½ cups water in a small skillet and bring to a boil over high heat. Stir in the tomato paste, remaining ¼ teaspoon salt, and black pepper and turn the heat down to a simmer.

7. When the oil is hot, add the fish (working in batches if needed to avoid crowding the pan) and fry until golden brown, about 3 minutes per side. Transfer to a wire rack to drain.

8. To serve, scoop a few spoonfuls of cou-cou onto each plate and smother with gravy. Place a piece of fish on the cou-cou and drizzle some more gravy on top.

6 mild white fish fillets, such as flying fish, flounder, or snapper

1¼ teaspoons iodized salt, divided

Juice of ½ lime

1½ teaspoons jerk seasoning, such as Walkerswood

4½ cups water, divided

8–12 fresh okra, trimmed and sliced into rounds

1 cup fine cornmeal

All-purpose flour, for dredging

½ cup vegetable oil

½ small yellow onion, thinly sliced

1 teaspoon fresh oregano leaves

Leaves from 6 thyme sprigs

1 tablespoon tomato paste

¼ teaspoon ground black pepper

Gambas al Ajillo

Garlic Shrimp

When I was growing up in the Philippines, if gambas al ajillo was on the menu when my family went out to dinner, I would have to order it. I always thought that gambas was a Filipino dish—which it is—but later realized it was based on a recipe from Spain (Filipino food is heavily influenced by Spanish cuisine). I always ate it with bread, but now I like to sometimes pair it with rice. My son loves shrimp and garlic, so I make this dish a lot—I just leave out the red pepper flakes for him because he likes it less spicy.

Serves 3–4 as an appetizer, 2 as a main

⅓ cup olive oil

6 garlic cloves, thinly sliced

1 pound peeled and deveined large shrimp (tails on or off)

Salt to taste

Pinch red pepper flakes, or to taste

½ teaspoon paprika

Juice of ½–1 lemon

Chopped fresh parsley, for garnish

Sliced crusty bread or steamed rice, for serving

1. In a sauté pan, heat the olive oil and thinly sliced garlic over medium heat. Cook, stirring occasionally, until the garlic is a light golden brown, 1–2 minutes. With a slotted spoon, remove the garlic to a paper towel to drain (reserve the oil in the pan). The garlic slices should be crispy like "chips."

2. Pat the shrimp dry and season with salt. Add the shrimp to the same pan with the garlic-infused oil and sear the shrimp on medium-high heat until it's mostly (but not fully) cooked, 2–3 minutes on each side. Transfer the shrimp to a plate (reserve the oil in the pan).

3. Reduce the heat to low. Season the oil with the red pepper flakes and paprika and cook, stirring, for 30 seconds.

4. Turn off the heat. Return the shrimp to the pan, sprinkle with the lemon juice and salt, and toss everything together.

5. Transfer the shrimp to a serving bowl and pour the pan sauce on top. Garnish with the garlic chips and parsley. Serve with bread or steamed rice.

Shrimp and Grits

I grew up eating grits, which were a household staple that my family brought with them from Mississippi to Ohio. When I moved to South Carolina, I was reintroduced to grits. Adding bacon, scallions, and other ingredients to the traditional Southern dish shrimp and grits made it my own: an homage to my family as well as my growth in my culinary journey. **Serves 6**

Shrimp and stock

2 cups water

3 pounds medium shrimp, peeled and deveined, tails removed and reserved

1 celery stalk, chopped

1 onion, chopped

1 teaspoon onion powder

1 teaspoon garlic powder

1 tablespoon salt, plus more for seasoning

1½ teaspoons ground black pepper, plus more for seasoning

1 tablespoon dried thyme

1 tablespoon paprika

1 teaspoon cayenne pepper

1 teaspoon plus a pinch seafood seasoning, such as Old Bay

2 tablespoons olive oil

1 tablespoon unsalted butter

Grits

4 cups water

1 cup heavy cream

5 tablespoons salted butter, divided

1 tablespoon salt

2 teaspoons ground black pepper

3 cups grits

1 cup shredded white cheddar cheese

Gravy

3 teaspoons olive oil, divided

1 pound precooked spiral ham, with glaze, chopped

1 red bell pepper, very finely chopped

1 green bell pepper, very finely chopped

2 garlic cloves, very finely chopped

3 scallions, 2 very finely chopped and 1 roughly chopped

8 ounces bacon

1. To make the shrimp stock, bring the water to a boil in a medium saucepan over high heat. Add the shrimp tails, celery, onion, onion powder, garlic powder, salt, black pepper, thyme, paprika, cayenne, and 1 teaspoon seafood seasoning and boil for 10–15 minutes. Strain the stock through a fine-mesh strainer. Set aside.

2. Meanwhile, to make the grits, in another medium saucepan, bring the water, cream, 3 tablespoons of the butter, the salt, and pepper to a boil over medium heat. Add the grits and cook, stirring continuously, for 15 minutes. Remove from the heat and stir in the cheddar and remaining 2 tablespoons butter until incorporated. Set aside.

3. To make the gravy, heat 2 teaspoons of the olive oil in a large skillet over medium heat. Add the ham and about 1 tablespoon of the glaze and sear the ham for 5–10 minutes. Be careful not to burn the glaze; add a little water if it gets too sticky. Add the shrimp stock to deglaze the pan. Turn the heat down to low. Add the bell peppers, garlic, and finely chopped scallions and simmer for 15 minutes.

(recipe continues)

4. Meanwhile, heat the remaining 1 teaspoon olive oil in another large skillet over medium heat. Add the bacon and fry until crisp, then drain on paper towels. Roughly chop the bacon. Wipe out the skillet.

5. To make the shrimp, heat the olive oil and butter in the now-empty skillet. Season the shrimp with salt, pepper, and a pinch of seafood seasoning. Add the shrimp to the skillet and cook until fully cooked, flipping halfway through, about 7 minutes. Add the shrimp to the gravy.

6. To serve, scoop ½–¾ cup grits into each bowl. Ladle some of the gravy on top of the grits, including 5–6 shrimp. Garnish with the bacon and roughly chopped scallion.

Cod Cake with Amba Sauce and Israeli Salad

BRAD

When I was growing up on the Jersey Shore, fish was a staple protein in our community and household. I like to use cod for my fish cakes, but using what looks freshest at your local market is paramount. This dish represents my coastal upbringing while also embracing my Middle Eastern roots with the pairing of an Israeli salad and tahini and amba dipping sauce. Amba is a spicy pickled mango sauce that's common across India and the Middle East. If you can't find it in local stores, you can buy it online. **Serves 6–8**

1. Heat 1 tablespoon of the oil in a sauté pan over medium heat. Add the onions and sauté until soft but not browned, about 5 minutes. Add the garlic and cook until fragrant. Set aside to cool.

2. Beat 2 of the eggs in a large bowl. Add the dill, parsley, cumin, cardamom, caraway, turmeric, cayenne, paprika, salt, lime zest and juice, cooled onions, and 1 cup of the panko. Add the cod and mayo and gently combine. Form the mixture into 6–8 equal patties, place on a plate, and refrigerate for at least 20 minutes.

3. Prepare three bowls for breading: one with the flour; one with the remaining 1 egg, beaten; and one with the remaining 2 cups panko. Coat each patty first with flour, then egg, and finally panko.

4. Heat ¼ cup of the oil in a large skillet over medium heat until a bread crumb dropped in the pan sizzles. Add half of the fish patties and fry until golden, about 5 minutes on each side, then transfer to a plate. Repeat with the remaining ¼ cup oil and remaining patties. Serve over rice, with amba dipping sauce and Israeli salad (recipes follow).

½ cup plus 1 tablespoon vegetable oil, divided

1 red onion, chopped

1 yellow onion, chopped

1 bulb head garlic, cloves separated, peeled, and minced

3 large eggs

1 cup chopped fresh dill

1 cup chopped fresh parsley

1½ tablespoons ground cumin

1½ tablespoons ground cardamom

1½ tablespoons ground caraway

1 teaspoon ground turmeric

1 teaspoon cayenne pepper

1 teaspoon paprika

1 tablespoon kosher salt

Grated zest and juice of 2 limes

3 cups panko bread crumbs, divided

3 pounds cod fillets, skin removed, minced

½ cup mayonnaise

1 cup all-purpose flour

Cooked white rice, for serving

(recipe continues)

★ Amba Sauce ★

½ cup tahini

1 cup mayonnaise

½ cup jarred amba

3 Israeli pickles, chopped (optional)

1. In a small bowl, combine the tahini, mayo, and amba and mix well. Stir in the chopped pickles, if desired.

★ Israeli Salad ★

2 Persian cucumbers, roughly chopped

2 Jersey tomatoes, roughly chopped

1 red onion, roughly chopped

½ cup chopped fresh parsley

Juice of 1 lemon

2 tablespoons olive oil

1 tablespoon sumac

1 teaspoon kosher salt

Ground black pepper to taste

1. Combine the cucumbers, tomatoes, onion, and parsley in a large bowl. Drizzle with the lemon juice and oil and season with the sumac, salt, and pepper.

———————

Fry Bake and Pink Salmon

SALMAH

Guyanese "bake" is a popular breakfast item, a fluffy fried hollow bread that's usually made for weekend brunch. I remember my mom would make the bake dough, cover it, and let it rest overnight. We'd be awakened by the smell of sweet bake frying. Inside a shiny bowl covered with a tea towel would be rows of round, warm bake. We'd quickly grab one to eat while slicing another open to fill with stewed pink salmon. The sweet bake and savory salmon is the best way to start the weekend—a tradition I carry on. **Makes about 25 bakes; serves 8**

Bakes

⅓ cup packed brown sugar

2 teaspoons white sugar

1 cup warm water

3½ cups all-purpose flour, plus more for dusting

1 tablespoon baking powder

½ teaspoon salt

2 tablespoons unsalted butter, softened

Vegetable oil, for drizzling and frying

Stewed pink salmon

2 tablespoons olive oil

1 wiri wiri pepper, minced

1 large yellow onion, chopped

3 large garlic cloves, grated

3 culantro sprigs, chopped

2 Roma tomatoes, diced

2 (14.75-ounce) cans pink salmon

2 tablespoons dried thyme

½ teaspoon ground black pepper

½ teaspoon paprika

¼ teaspoon garlic powder

Salt to taste

1 teaspoon tomato paste

¼–1 cup water (if needed)

2 scallions, finely chopped (optional)

Hot sauce, for serving (optional)

1. To make the bakes, in a small bowl, dissolve the sugars in the warm water and set aside.

2. In a large bowl, whisk together the flour, baking powder, and salt. Add the butter and rub it into the dry ingredients with your fingers.

3. Make a well in the center of the dry ingredients and pour in the sugar water. Using a silicone spatula, gently combine the dry ingredients with the sugar water, bringing the ingredients together to form a soft ball of dough.

4. Transfer the dough to a lightly floured surface and knead for 3 minutes, just until the dough is smooth and soft. Drizzle a bit of oil over the dough and cover it with a damp cloth. Let it rest for 20 minutes.

5. In a large skillet, heat about ½ inch oil over medium-high heat to 350 degrees F. Set a wire rack over a rimmed baking sheet.

6. Roll out the dough on a floured surface to about ⅛ inch thick. Cut as many 6-inch bakes as you can out of the dough. Gather and reroll the scraps as needed.

7. Once the oil is up to temperature, fry the bakes for 1–2 minutes. The bakes should puff and rise in the oil. Use a spoon to pour oil over each piece of dough to help it puff. Flip the bakes over and continue to fry until golden brown on both sides. Transfer the bakes to the wire rack to cool. (Cooled bakes can be stored in an airtight container at room temperature until ready to serve.)

8. To make the salmon and gravy, in a large skillet , heat the oil over medium heat. Add the wiri-wiri pepper, onion, garlic, and culantro and sauté, stirring frequently, until fragrant, about 5 minutes. Add the tomatoes and sauté for 2 minutes. Add the salmon and cook, stirring, for 10 minutes. Add the thyme, black pepper, paprika, garlic powder, salt, and tomato paste and sauté for 5–10 minutes, stirring often. If the mixture is dry, add water, ¼ cup at a time. Cook until everything is well combined and a gravy has formed, 7–10 more minutes.

9. To serve, cut each bake in half. Spoon in some of the stewed salmon and gravy and garnish with scallions and hot sauce, if desired.

Seared Ahi with Smashed Avocado and Pineapple Salsa

GRAHAM

I am a firm believer in the philosophy of less is more, as well as letting great ingredients simply taste like themselves. Taking ahi tuna straight from the ocean, gently searing it, and serving it with smashed avocado and a simple pineapple salsa just makes sense. Rich and fatty go alongside sweet and tart, and the whole plate is rounded out by an amazing piece of fish. Because I am an avid fisherman, this dish is near and dear to my heart. **Serves 4**

Vegetable oil, for frying

4 (4-ounce) ahi tuna steaks

Salt and ground black pepper to taste

2 avocados

2 limes

2 cups diced pineapple

1 cup minced red bell pepper

1 cup minced red onion

1 jalapeño pepper, minced

½ bunch cilantro, chopped

1. Place a large skillet over high heat and coat the bottom with oil. Pat the ahi steaks dry and season both sides with salt and pepper. Sear the steaks for 20–30 seconds on each side to gain a bit of golden-brown color on the outside while maintaining a rare center. Remove the ahi steaks to a plate to rest.

2. Slice the avocados lengthwise and remove the pits. Scoop the avocado flesh into a bowl. Squeeze the juice of 1 lime over the avocados and season with salt and pepper. Use a fork to mash and mix the avocado to the desired consistency.

3. Combine the pineapple, bell pepper, onion, jalapeño, and cilantro in a medium bowl. Add the juice of the other lime and season with salt and pepper. Mix gently to combine, then taste and season again if necessary.

4. Thinly slice each of the ahi steaks, keeping the slices together until you are ready to plate. To plate, place a few spoonfuls of avocado mash in the center of each plate and spread into a circle with the back of a spoon. Place the sliced ahi on top of the smashed avocado, then gently shingle the slices to expose the rare center. Spoon the pineapple salsa over the ahi and around the sides of the smashed avocado.

Cod in Saffron Cream Sauce

BRAD

Inspired by an amazing dish I had during one of my many trips to Israel, this creamy and spicy white fish, served over rice, is simple yet packed with flavor. The saffron makes it a real showstopper, giving the dish not only an incredibly beautiful color but also a rich flavor, which pairs beautifully with the cream and the spiciness of the hot peppers. **Serves 6**

1½ cups short-grain white rice

2 cups water

1 (2-ounce) can anchovies packed in olive oil

10 garlic cloves, peeled

3 green chiles, minced

¼ teaspoon kosher salt

1 tablespoon extra virgin olive oil

½ cup minced shallots

2 tablespoons high-acid dry white wine

1 quart heavy cream

2 red chiles, 1 chopped, 1 thinly sliced

2 tablespoons crushed Persian saffron

¼ teaspoon black pepper

1 bunch parsley, chopped

6 (6-ounce) thick center-cut cod fillets

1. Combine the rice and water in a medium saucepan and bring to a boil over high heat. Reduce the heat to low, cover, and simmer for 20 minutes, or until all the water is absorbed. Let stand for 10 minutes before serving.

2. Meanwhile, in a small food processor or blender, make a paste with the anchovies and their oil, garlic, green chiles, and salt. Set aside.

3. In a large sauté pan, heat the olive oil over medium heat. Add the shallots and sauté until soft, about 5 minutes. Add the anchovy-garlic paste, reduce the heat to medium-low, and cook for 1 minute. Add the white wine and let simmer for 2–3 minutes. Add the cream, chopped red chiles, saffron, and pepper and adjust the seasoning to taste. Stir in the parsley.

4. Add the fish and cook until cooked through (145 degrees F), 15–20 minutes.

5. Serve the cod and sauce with the rice. Garnish with sliced red chile.

Rice, Pasta, and Casseroles

Thai Crab Fried Rice 175

**Jerk Alfredo Pasta and Pan-Seared
Scallops with Side Salad** 176

Cavatappi Pollo 179

Chicken Hekka with Wontons 180

Beef Kokkinisto with Macaronada 183
(Braised Beef in Red Sauce with Pasta)

Japchae with Bean Sprout Salad 184
(Stir-Fried Glass Noodles with Beef and Vegetables)

Pastitsio 187
(Baked Pasta with Meat and Béchamel)

Tagliatelle Bolognese 188

Sweet Noodle Kugel 191

Nukides 194
(Libyan Gnocchi with Stewed Lamb)

Thai Crab Fried Rice

This is one of my favorite street food dishes in Thailand. It's so popular you can find it everywhere from street carts to restaurants that serve nothing else. One of the best places to get this dish is at the Michelin-starred Jay Fai, where the chef cooks every single dish herself. It's very hard to get a reservation there, but my husband and I were lucky enough to get in the last time we were in Bangkok. Here is my version of the dish, which is so simple it comes together in just a few minutes but delivers lots of flavor thanks to umami-rich fish sauce (a must for Thai fried rice) and delicate crab. **Serves 2**

LEAH

1. Heat the oil in a large nonstick sauté pan over medium heat. Add the garlic and scallion whites and sauté for 2 minutes, or until fragrant and the garlic begins to turn golden. Push the garlic and scallions to one side of the pan.

2. Add the eggs to the other side of the pan. Break them up a little with a spoon to scramble them slightly, then let them set. Add the rice and stir-fry for 2 minutes.

3. Season with the soy sauce, fish sauce, sugar, MSG (if using), salt, and white pepper. Stir-fry for 2–3 minutes, until everything is well incorporated. Add the crabmeat and scallion greens and stir to warm through.

4. Garnish with cucumber slices and cilantro. Serve with a lime wedge to squeeze over the top of each bowl.

3 tablespoons vegetable oil

2 tablespoons minced garlic

3 scallions, sliced, green and white parts separated

2 large eggs

3 cups cooked and cooled white rice

2 tablespoons soy sauce

1½ tablespoons fish sauce

1½ teaspoons sugar

Pinch MSG (optional)

Salt to taste

¼ teaspoon white pepper

8 ounces jumbo lump crabmeat, picked over

Cucumber slices, for garnish

Cilantro leaves, for garnish

Lime wedges, for serving

Jerk Alfredo Pasta and Pan–Seared Scallops with Side Salad

LEANNA

I absolutely love pasta and cheese individually; but when they come together, they make my heart dance. Now add jerk seasoning for a little heat, perfectly seared scallops, and a side salad (so I can pretend that this isn't really overindulgence) and it becomes a seafood and pasta lover's dream. The only thing that could make this creamy, spicy pasta dish better is if I were enjoying it sitting seaside, watching the tide gently roll in. **Serves 6**

Jerk Alfredo pasta

2 teaspoons extra virgin olive oil, divided

1 teaspoon salt, plus more for seasoning

8 ounces linguine

8 tablespoons (1 stick) unsalted butter

1 cup heavy cream

2 cups (5 ounces) grated Parmesan cheese

Ground black pepper to taste

2 garlic cloves, minced

½–1 teaspoon jerk seasoning (mild or hot)

1 small red onion, julienned

6 baby sweet peppers or 1 small red bell pepper, seeded and julienned

2 cups baby spinach

Pan-seared scallops

12 large scallops

Coarse sea salt and ground black pepper

2 tablespoons extra virgin olive oil

2 teaspoons herbed butter

2 garlic cloves, minced

3 thyme sprigs

½ cup Pinot Grigio or other dry white wine

Sliced scallions, for garnish

Chopped fresh cilantro or parsley, for garnish

1. Bring a large pot of water to a boil over high heat. Add 1 teaspoon of the olive oil, the salt, and pasta. Cook until the pasta is al dente, 8–9 minutes. Reserve ½ cup of the cooking water, then drain the pasta and immediately run it under cool water. Drain again and set aside.

2. While the pasta cooks, make the Alfredo sauce. In a small saucepan, melt the butter over medium-high heat. Add the cream. Once the cream is heated, reduce the heat. Add the cheese and stir until melted. If the sauce is a little too thick, add a little pasta water to thin it out to the desired consistency. Season with salt and pepper as desired.

3. In a large skillet, heat the remaining 1 teaspoon olive oil over medium heat. Add the garlic and cook until lightly browned, 1–2 minutes. Stir in the Alfredo sauce and jerk seasoning. Using a pair of tongs, mix in the linguine, coating it thoroughly in the sauce. Stir for about 2 minutes, then turn the heat to medium-low. Add the onion and peppers and mix them into the pasta with the tongs. Add the spinach and stir to combine. Allow the pasta mixture to simmer for 2–3 minutes, then turn off the heat.

4. Using a paper towel, pat the scallops dry on both sides. (You will not get a good sear if the scallops are soaking wet.) Liberally season both sides of the scallops with salt and pepper.

5. In a cast iron skillet, heat the olive oil over medium-high heat. Carefully place the scallops in the skillet. Sear on one side for 2–2½ minutes, then flip and sear on the other side for 2 minutes. Transfer the scallops to serving plates.

6. Turn the heat down to medium. Add the herbed butter and garlic and stir until browned. Add the thyme sprigs and stir, then add the wine, using a wooden spoon to scrape the crust from the bottom of the pan.

7. Plate the pasta with the scallops. Spoon the butter-wine sauce over the scallops. Garnish with scallions and cilantro and serve immediately, with a side salad (recipe on the next page).

★ Side Salad ★

1–2 garlic cloves, minced

¾ cup extra virgin olive oil

¼ cup balsamic vinegar

1 teaspoon Italian seasoning

Iodized salt and ground black pepper to taste

1 large carrot, peeled

1 (5-ounce) bag spring mix

1 large English cucumber, thinly sliced

1 red onion, thinly sliced

1. In a small bowl, whisk together the garlic, olive oil, balsamic vinegar, and Italian seasoning until fully incorporated. Season with salt and pepper.

2. Using a vegetable peeler, peel the carrot into ribbons. Combine the spring mix, carrot ribbons, cucumber, and red onion in a large bowl. Pour the desired amount of dressing over the salad, using tongs to help evenly distribute the dressing; be careful not to overdress the salad. Serve immediately.

Cavatappi Pollo

TED

For my first date with my now-wife Tina, I took her to my favorite little pasta place in Lincoln Park in Chicago. This restaurant had been my go-to for years and I had a favorite dish on the menu that I always ordered. Of course when it was time to order, Tina chose my favorite dish, the cavatappi pollo: pasta with chicken, mushrooms, and sun-dried tomatoes in cream sauce. I didn't want to order the same thing, so I quickly pivoted and ordered something else without telling her she picked my favorite. We began dating regularly and I wanted to make her this dish for dinner at home on one of our dates, so I practiced it a few times to get it just right. When I finally made it for her, I told her how she ordered my favorite dish on our first date, so I wanted to make it special for her. This recipe makes enough to feed six people, but it can easily be halved for your next date night (with some pasta left over to enjoy the next day). **Serves 6**

1. Heat 1½ teaspoons of the olive oil and the tomato oil in a large skillet over medium-high heat. Season the chicken breasts with the Italian seasoning, salt, and pepper, then add the chicken to the pan and sauté until it is cooked through and no longer pink, 6–8 minutes per side. Transfer the chicken to a plate.

2. Heat the remaining 1½ teaspoons olive oil in the same pan, still over medium-high heat. Add the mushrooms and sauté until lightly browned on the edges and tender, 3–4 minutes. Transfer the mushrooms to the plate with the chicken.

3. In a medium bowl, whisk together the cream, cornstarch, and Parmesan. Add the cream mixture to the pan, lower the heat to medium, and whisk the mixture until it comes to a simmer. Let it simmer until it is thickened, 15–20 minutes.

4. While the cream mixture is simmering, bring a large pot of water to a boil over high heat. Generously salt the boiling water, then add the pasta. Cook the pasta until al dente, 9–10 minutes or the recommended time on the box. Drain the pasta and return it to the pot.

5. While the pasta is cooking, add the sun-dried tomatoes to the thickened cream sauce. Return the chicken and mushrooms to the pan and stir to coat everything evenly with the sauce.

6. Pour the chicken and cream sauce mixture into the pot of pasta and stir to combine everything thoroughly. Spoon portions of pasta and chicken into serving dishes and garnish with the parsley.

3 teaspoons olive oil, divided

¾ cup sun-dried tomatoes, roughly chopped, plus 1½ teaspoons sun-dried tomato oil

2 large boneless, skinless chicken breasts, cut into bite-size pieces

1½ teaspoons Italian seasoning

Salt and ground black pepper to taste

3 (8-ounce) packages baby bella (cremini) mushrooms, sliced

3 cups heavy cream

1½ tablespoons cornstarch

1 cup grated Parmesan cheese

2 (1-pound) boxes cavatappi pasta

1 bunch parsley, chopped, for garnish

Chicken Hekka with Wontons

It seems that just about every culture has a noodle dish to call its own. Chicken hekka is one from Hawai'i: tender chicken stir-fried with delicious vegetables and tossed with rice noodles in a slightly sweet yet salty sauce. I serve it alongside crispy, flavor-packed filled wontons. This is the ultimate comfort food. **Serves 6**

2 tablespoons vegetable oil

2 pounds boneless, skinless chicken thighs, cut into large pieces

Salt and ground black pepper to taste

1-inch piece ginger, sliced

1 cup shoyu or soy sauce

½ cup packed brown sugar

1 (8-ounce) can bamboo shoots, drained

1 cup dried shiitake mushrooms, soaked and sliced

1 large carrot, peeled and julienned

1 small onion, sliced

5 ounces bean thread rice noodles

2 scallions, sliced

1. Heat the oil in a large pot over medium-high heat. Add the chicken, salt, and pepper and cook, stirring, until the chicken is slightly browned, 10–12 minutes. Add the ginger and continue to cook, stirring, until the chicken is cooked through, 5–10 minutes.

2. In a small bowl, mix the shoyu and brown sugar until well combined. Add the shoyu mixture to the pot of chicken, along with the bamboo shoots, mushrooms, carrot, and onion. Continue to cook until all the vegetables are softened, 5–10 minutes.

3. Meanwhile, bring a medium pot of water to a boil over high heat. Add the noodles and cook according to the package instructions, usually a minute or two. Drain and set aside.

4. Once the chicken has cooked through and the vegetables have softened, add the noodles and stir to combine. Garnish with the scallions and serve with wontons (recipe follows).

(recipe continues)

★ Wontons ★

Vegetable oil, for frying

4 ounces ground beef

4 ounces ground pork

¼ cup diced kamaboko (see note)

¼ cup diced water chestnuts

2 tablespoons chopped scallion

1 teaspoon minced garlic

½ teaspoon salt

½ teaspoon ground black pepper

24 wonton wrappers

3 tablespoons hot mustard powder, such as S&B

3 tablespoons shoyu or soy sauce

Note: Kamaboko, or fish cake, is a processed seafood product that's common in Japanese cooking. It's made by forming white fish with flavorings into loaves and steaming until firm. Pink or red-skinned kamaboko is widely available at grocery stores in Hawai'i. If you can't find it locally, look online.

1. In a wok, large pot, or deep fryer, heat about 1 inch of oil over medium-high heat to 350 degrees F.

2. In a large bowl, combine the beef, pork, kamaboko, water chestnuts, scallion, garlic, salt, and pepper. Mix well.

3. Place a heaping tablespoon of the meat mixture in the center of a wonton wrapper. Use your fingertip to spread a small amount of water along two edges of the wonton wrapper. Bring the opposite corners together, forming a triangle, and firmly press the edges to seal. Repeat to form the remaining wontons.

4. Working in batches, gently lower the wontons into the hot oil and fry until golden brown, 1–2 minutes each side. Transfer the wontons to paper towels to drain.

5. In a small bowl, whisk together the mustard powder and shoyu. Serve the wontons immediately, with the mustard dipping sauce.

Beef Kokkinisto with Macaronada (Makaronia)

TED

Braised Beef in Red Sauce with Pasta

Greece is a geographically diverse country with vast coastlines that provide it with an abundance of the seafood that is a well-known part of its cuisine. However, many parts of mainland Greece are in the mountains, where varying meats such as lamb, goat, and veal make up the regular diet. Kokkinisto is beef braised in tomato sauce with a variety of spices, served over a macaroni-style long noodle. When I was growing up, my mom, Nancy, would make this as our "spaghetti and meatballs." When my mom was diagnosed with cancer, she was very limited in how often she cooked, and this recipe was almost lost to history until my sister, Annette, found it several years after our mom passed away. I started making it for my family and my oldest daughter, Sienna, fell in love with it! It has become a regular dish at our dinner table. **Serves 6**

1. Season the tri-tip all over with salt and pepper. Set an Instant Pot to sauté. Add 1 tablespoon of the olive oil and, when it is hot, sear the meat on all sides. Transfer the tri-tip to a plate.

2. Add the remaining 1 tablespoon olive oil to the Instant Pot and, when it is hot, sauté the onion until it is almost translucent, about 5 minutes. Add the garlic, carrots, tomato paste, crushed tomatoes, sugar, chicken stock, and cinnamon and stir. Season with salt and pepper.

3. Return the tri-tip to the pot and pour in enough water to cover the meat. Close the lid and set to sealing. Cook on high pressure for 35 minutes. Release the pressure manually, press "cancel," and remove the lid.

4. Transfer the meat to a cutting board. Strain the liquid and pour it into a small saucepan. Cook on the stovetop over high heat until reduced and slightly thickened, about 10 minutes.

5. Meanwhile, bring a large pot of water to a boil over high heat. Cook the pasta according to the package instructions. Drain.

6. Cut the meat into 1-inch pieces. Divide the pasta equally among six bowls. Serve three pieces of meat per bowl, topped with the sauce.

1 (2-pound) tri-tip beef roast

Salt and ground black pepper to taste

2 tablespoons Greek olive oil, divided

1½ cups chopped yellow onion

3 garlic cloves, minced

1 cup sliced carrots

1 tablespoon tomato paste

1 (28-ounce) can crushed tomatoes

1 tablespoon sugar

2 cups chicken stock

½ cinnamon stick

1 (1-pound) package thick macaroni or bucatini, such as Misko

Japchae with Bean Sprout Salad

Stir-Fried Glass Noodles with Beef and Vegetables

KHELA

My friend Shannon started a local food group that altered the trajectory of my life. From this group I've grown a foodie "framily" of cherished friends. Shannon hosted a giant annual garlic contest. An original painting by her husband, renowned local artist Rich Bowman, was the coveted prize for winning. With nearly one hundred folks (mostly foodies) voting, the dishes needed to be creative and tasty. I saw the sweet potato noodles at my favorite Asian grocery and had to try them. Japchae, the Korean beef and noodle dish with veggies, was like nothing I'd had before. For the contest, I used beef tenderloin, upped the garlic and heat to please the party palates, and won! This dish can also be prepared with different proteins and/or veggies. With a fresh bean sprout salad on the side, it's a guaranteed crowd-pleaser. Sadly, Shannon passed away from a rare cancer, so that first time I made japchae is an especially cherished memory. **Serves 6**

Beef

1 tablespoon dark soy sauce

1 teaspoon mirin

1 teaspoon toasted sesame oil

2 garlic cloves, grated

½ teaspoon ground black pepper

6 ounces beef tenderloin, thinly sliced

Sauce

¼ cup dark soy sauce

1 tablespoon packed brown sugar

1 tablespoon honey

1 tablespoon toasted sesame oil

¼ teaspoon ground black pepper

Japchae

3 large eggs

2 tablespoons vegetable oil, divided

1 onion, sliced

2 carrots, peeled and julienned

1 red bell pepper, seeded and sliced

4 ounces shiitake mushrooms, sliced

6 ounces baby spinach

1 (16-ounce) bag sweet potato starch noodles

2 tablespoons toasted sesame seeds, for garnish

2 tablespoons toasted sesame oil, for garnish

Korean hot sauce, for serving (optional)

---

1. To marinate the beef, in a large bowl, whisk together the soy sauce, mirin, sesame oil, garlic, and pepper. Add the beef and toss to coat. Set aside.

2. To make the sauce, in a small bowl, whisk together the soy sauce, brown sugar, honey, sesame oil, and pepper. Set aside.

3. To make the egg garnish, in a medium bowl, whisk the eggs until completely blended. Heat 1 tablespoon of the oil in a small nonstick skillet over medium-high heat. Pour in the egg mixture and cook without touching until it is set. Flip the egg and cook on the other side until it is cooked though but has not taken on any color. Transfer the egg to a plate to cool, then cut into strips. Set aside.

4. In a large nonstick or cast iron skillet, heat the remaining 1 tablespoon oil over medium-high heat. Add the onion and cook, stirring, for 1 minute. Add the carrots and cook, stirring, for 2 minutes.

Transfer the onion and carrots to a large serving bowl. Add the red bell pepper to the skillet and cook, stirring, for 5–8 minutes, then add it to the bowl with the onion and carrots. Add the mushrooms and cook, stirring, for 5–8 minutes, then transfer to the bowl. Add the spinach and cook just until it wilts, 3–4 minutes, then transfer to the bowl.

5. Bring a large pot of water to a boil over high heat. Add the noodles and cook according to the package instructions, usually 6–7 minutes. Drain the noodles, then add them to the bowl of vegetables.

6. Heat the same skillet over high heat. Add the meat and sear for 1–2 minutes on each side, just until it's no longer pink on the outside (or to the desired doneness). Add the steak to the bowl of noodles and vegetables, along with the sauce, and mix until everything is evenly combined.

7. Top the japchae with the egg garnish, toasted sesame seeds, and a drizzle of sesame oil. Serve with Korean hot sauce, if you like, and a side of bean sprout salad (below).

№ 2 | Bean Sprout Salad

1 pound soybean or mung bean sprouts

3 garlic cloves, grated

3 tablespoons chopped scallion

1–2 tablespoons Korean red chili flakes

1 tablespoon toasted sesame seeds

1 tablespoon toasted sesame oil

½–1 teaspoon soy sauce (not dark)

½ teaspoon salt

1. Bring a large pot of water to a boil over high heat. Add the sprouts and boil for 2–3 minutes. Drain, then spin the sprouts in a salad spinner to drain off all excess water.

2. Put the sprouts in a large bowl. Add the garlic, scallion, chili flakes, toasted sesame seeds, sesame oil, soy sauce, and salt and stir to combine. Chill until ready to serve.

Pastitsio

Baked Pasta with Meat and Béchamel

TED

Pastitsio is a savory meat mixture with a creamy béchamel sauce and noodles, served in a large baking dish. The combination makes this dish perfect for large family holiday gatherings. My mom, Nancy, always made this dish for major holidays and it was a fixture in my life growing up. As an adult, after my parents passed away, I started making this recipe to make sure to carry on their legacy for my children and the rest of my family. This dish exemplifies how food brings families together, keeps them strong, and carries on traditions. **Serves 8 to 10**

1. Preheat the oven to 350 degrees F.

2. Bring a large pot of water to a boil over high heat. Add the pasta and cook according to the package instructions. Drain and return the pasta to the pot, then drizzle with olive oil and cover the pot.

3. Heat the vegetable oil in a large skillet over medium heat. Add the onion and garlic and cook until lightly browned, 5–7 minutes. Add the tomato paste, crushed tomatoes, ground beef, cinnamon, nutmeg, cloves, and red wine. Simmer for 15–20 minutes.

4. In a medium saucepan, melt the butter over medium heat. Add the milk, ½ cup of the cheese, and the farina and cook until thickened, 5–7 minutes. Do not allow to boil. Once the mixture is starting to thicken up, add the egg yolks.

5. Lay the noodles in a 13 × 9-inch baking dish. For visual effect when the pastitsio is sliced, arrange them so they are all going in the same direction. Spread the meat mixture over the noodles. Sprinkle half of the remaining cheese on the meat. Spread the cream sauce over the top, then sprinkle with the remaining cheese.

6. Bake for 50–60 minutes, until golden brown on top. Cut into squares, garnish with parsley, and serve.

1 (12- to 16-ounce) package bucatini or thick macaroni, such as Misko

Olive oil, for drizzling

2 tablespoons vegetable oil

1 small red onion, chopped

1 garlic clove, grated

1 (6-ounce) can tomato paste

1 (28-ounce) can crushed tomatoes

1½ pounds ground beef

⅛ teaspoon ground cinnamon

Pinch ground nutmeg

Pinch ground cloves

¾ cup dry red wine

8 tablespoons (1 stick) unsalted butter

3 cups whole milk

1½ cups grated mizithra cheese

2–3 tablespoons farina, such as Cream of Wheat

2 large egg yolks

Chopped fresh parsley, for garnish

Tagliatelle Bolognese

MARIA

When I was twenty years old, I was traveling in Italy for a study abroad trip. I knew there was so much to an Italian Bolognese that I was missing in America. I walked down the arcades of Bologna, found the tiniest trattoria, and ordered the dish I had hyped up in my head for months. I wondered if it could live up to the expectations I had conjured in my mind. And it did. This dish made me obsess over cooking with new textures. After about a decade of tinkering with this recipe, I think I created a Bolognese that lives up to the version I had on that late summer night in Bologna so many years ago. **Serves 10**

1 large white onion, roughly chopped

2 bunches celery, roughly chopped

2–3 carrots, peeled and roughly chopped

½ cup vegetable oil

2 pounds ground beef (80–85% lean)

Salt to taste

4 ounces pancetta, diced

1–2 tablespoons dry white wine to taste

1 (4.5-ounce) tube tomato paste

1–2 bay leaves

Pinch ground nutmeg

3 cups beef stock

1 cup milk

2 (1-pound) boxes tagliatelle pasta

½ cup grated Parmesan cheese, plus more for serving

Chopped fresh basil, for garnish

1. Pulse the onion, celery, and carrots in a food processor until very finely chopped. Transfer to a medium bowl.

2. Heat the oil in a Dutch oven over medium heat. Add the ground beef, lightly season with salt, and cook, stirring often to break up the meat, until no longer pink, 6–8 minutes. Transfer the beef to a large bowl.

3. Wipe out the pot, then add the pancetta. Cook over medium heat for 6–8 minutes, stirring often. Add the vegetable mixture to the pot and cook, stirring occasionally, until the vegetables are very soft and beginning to stick to the surface, 6–8 minutes.

4. Return the beef to the pot and add the white wine. Reduce the heat to medium-low and simmer until the wine has evaporated and the meat is finely broken up, 12–15 minutes.

5. Add the tomato paste, bay leaf, and nutmeg and cook, stirring occasionally, until the tomato paste is slightly darkened, about 5 minutes.

6. Add the beef stock and milk and season with salt if needed. Reduce the heat to the lowest setting and let simmer 20–30 minutes while you make the pasta.

7. Fill a large pot with water and salt generously. Bring to a boil over high heat. Add the pasta and cook until 1 or 2 minutes shy of al dente. Reserve 1 cup of the cooking water, then drain.

8. Transfer the pasta to the pot of sauce. Add the reserved pasta cooking water and Parmesan. Increase the heat to medium and bring the sauce back to a simmer. Cook, stirring constantly, until the pasta is al dente and the liquid is slightly thickened, about 2 minutes.

9. Serve the pasta and sauce in bowls, topped with more grated Parmesan and fresh basil.

Sweet Noodle Kugel
with Spinach Salad with Za'atar, Sumac, and Dates

ABBE

Kugels of all types are found on many Jewish tables. Whether they are potato or noodle, sweet or savory, it seems everyone has an opinion on kugel. As a child, my mom often made a noodle kugel as part of our Friday night Shabbat dinner. I must admit, her savory version was not my fave. As an adult I discovered a sweet version and soon after decided to create my own. It quickly became a hit in our home, and why wouldn't it? With its slightly sweet, creamy, raisin-studded interior and the crunchy, buttery cereal topping, it is a winner! Serve with a spinach salad with za'atar croutons. **Serves 8**

1. Preheat the oven to 350 degrees F. Generously butter eight 1½-cup ceramic souffle dishes. (A 13 × 9-inch glass baking dish may also be used.)

2. Bring a large pot of water to a boil over high heat. Add the salt and noodles and boil for no more than 7 minutes, so as to not overcook them. Drain the noodles, then return them to the pot and toss with 3 tablespoons of the butter.

3. In a microwave or on the stovetop, melt the remaining 3 tablespoons butter. Transfer to a large bowl and add the cream cheese and sugar. By hand or using an electric mixer, beat until smooth.

4. Add the eggs, sour cream, cottage cheese, and vanilla and beat until as smooth as possible. The cottage cheese will remain lumpy. Drain the golden raisins and add to the bowl. Add the noodles and mix well, stirring until completely combined.

5. Divide the noodle mixture into the prepared souffle dishes. Smooth the tops as much as possible. Crush the cornflakes slightly between your hands and sprinkle them over the noodle mixture until completely covered. Dot with more butter.

6. Bake for about 40 minutes, until the kugel feels firm and a knife inserted into the center comes out clean. The tops and edges should be golden, and there should be both crunchy and creamy parts.

7. Set aside to cool slightly, then serve with the spinach salad (recipe follows).

6 tablespoons unsalted butter, divided, plus more for greasing and dotting

1 tablespoon salt

1 (12-ounce) bag wide egg noodles

4 ounces cream cheese

⅓ cup sugar

3 large eggs

1 cup sour cream

1 pound small-curd cottage cheese

1 teaspoon vanilla extract

½ cup golden raisins or other dried fruit, plumped in 1 cup hot water if fruit is dry (optional)

½–1 cup cornflake cereal

(recipe continues)

★ Spinach Salad with Za'atar, Sumac, and Dates ★

3 tablespoons white wine vinegar

1 medium red onion, thinly sliced

¾ cup chopped dates or other dried fruit

½ teaspoon plus a pinch salt

4 tablespoons (½ stick) unsalted butter

2 tablespoons olive oil, plus more for seasoning

1 cup bite-size pieces artisanal Italian whole wheat bread or challah

1 cup sliced almonds

4 teaspoons za'atar

1 teaspoon red pepper flakes

8 cups baby spinach

¼ cup lemon juice as needed

1. Combine the vinegar, onion, and dates in a small bowl. Add a pinch of salt and let marinate for at least 20 minutes.

2. Meanwhile, in a medium skillet, melt the butter and olive oil together over medium heat. Add the bread and cook until golden and crispy, 8–10 minutes. Add the almonds at the end of the cooking time to toast them a little. Remove the mixture from the heat and mix in the za'atar, red pepper flakes, and ½ teaspoon salt. Set aside to cool.

3. In a large bowl, toss the spinach with the bread mixture. Add the date and red onion mixture, tossing to combine. Drizzle with the lemon juice. Taste the salad and add more olive oil, lemon juice, and/or salt if needed.

———————

Nukides

Libyan Gnocchi with Stewed Lamb

BRAD

Nukides are a Libyan version of gnocchi served with stewed lamb. Purchased premade gnocchi can be substituted if you prefer not to make your own. **Serves 6**

Stewed lamb

Vegetable oil, for cooking

2 pounds lamb stew meat (such as shoulder), cubed

1–2 marrow bones

1 (6-ounce) can tomato paste

1 (28-ounce) can whole tomatoes, chopped

1 (15-ounce) can tomato sauce

5 garlic cloves, minced

1½ tablespoons ground caraway

1½ tablespoons hot paprika

1½ tablespoons sweet paprika

1½ teaspoons cayenne pepper

Kosher salt and ground black pepper to taste

About 10 cups boiling water

Fresh cilantro leaves, for garnish

Chopped fresh chives, for garnish

Nukides

2 cups all-purpose flour, plus more for dusting

½ cup coarse semolina

1 teaspoon kosher salt

1 teaspoon ground black pepper

2 large eggs

2 tablespoons water

3 tablespoons vegetable oil

1. Coat the bottom of a Dutch oven with oil and heat over medium-high heat. Add the lamb and marrow bones and brown on all sides, 8–10 minutes per side. Add the tomato paste, chopped tomatoes with their juices, tomato sauce, garlic, caraway, both paprikas, and cayenne. Season with salt and black pepper. Allow the mixture to cook for 3–5 minutes to infuse the flavors and combine thoroughly.

2. Add enough boiling water so that the meat and tomatoes are just covered. Bring to a boil, then reduce the heat to a simmer and cook for 30 minutes.

3. Meanwhile, make the nukides. In a bowl, combine the flour, semolina, salt, pepper, eggs, water, and oil. Mix the dough with a wooden spoon or spatula until well combined, then use your hands to knead the dough together. The texture should be silky and slightly sticky and should hold its form if shaped. (If the dough feels too crumbly, you can add a little bit of water or oil.) Once the desired texture is achieved, let the dough rest in the bowl for 10 minutes.

4. Lightly dust a rimmed baking sheet with flour. On a lightly floured work surface, roll out the dough into long ropes about ½ inch in diameter. Using a butter knife or bench scraper, cut off chickpea-size pieces. Place the pieces on the floured baking sheet and set aside until ready to use.

5. After 30 minutes of stewing the meat and once the nukides are formed, add the dough pieces to the pot along with ½ cup water. Gently stir the stew to combine. Simmer the nukides and lamb stew for about 1 hour, stirring occasionally. Add more water as needed to make sure the sauce is not too thick.

6. To serve, remove the marrow bones. Ladle the stew into bowls and garnish with fresh cilantro and chives.

Desserts
and
Baked Goods

Best Macaroons Ever

(Apricot-Almond Dark Chocolate Macaroons and Piña Colada Macaroons)

ABBE

Macaroons are flourless coconut cookies that are often found on Passover tables. I have made them for many years, in countless varieties, and never know which one is my favorite—so here are two of my top flavor combinations: almond, apricot, and dark chocolate versus pineapple, macadamia nut, and white chocolate (I leave the amounts of ingredients flexible so you can adjust to your liking). Make as many as you want, because with just five base ingredients, you won't have to spend hours in the kitchen. Because they are so moist, they keep for a long time, but I promise they will disappear fast! **Makes about 45 macaroons**

1. Preheat the oven to 350 degrees F with a rack in the middle position. Line two rimmed baking sheets with parchment paper.

2. In a large bowl, whisk the egg whites and salt until frothy, 1–2 minutes. Add the sweetened condensed milk and vanilla and stir until well mixed. Using a silicone spatula, fold in the coconut, stirring until well blended. Divide the mixture evenly between two bowls.

3. Set one bowl of coconut mixture and a small bowl of water near your work surface. Dip your fingers into the bowl of water, then collect about 2 tablespoons of the coconut mixture in your hands. Pack it tight to get it to hold together. Place the balls about 1 inch apart on one of the prepared baking sheets. Press an indentation into the center of each ball for the apricot jam filling.

4. Stir the rum and pineapple into the second bowl of coconut mixture. Using the same method as before with a bowl of water, make 2-tablespoon balls of coconut mixture and place them on the other prepared baking sheet. Sprinkle the tops with the chopped macadamia nuts.

5. Bake both sheets of cookies for 10 minutes. Remove the first sheet from the oven. Spoon about 1 teaspoon apricot jam in the indentation in the center of each cookie. Sprinkle the tops with the sliced almonds. Return the cookies to the oven and continue baking both sheets for another 8–10 minutes, until golden brown. Let the cookies cool completely on their sheets.

6. In separate bowls, melt the dark chocolate and white chocolate in the microwave. Using a spoon, drizzle the melted dark chocolate over the apricot-almond macaroons. Drizzle the melted white chocolate over the pineapple-macadamia macaroons. Let the chocolate cool and set completely before serving.

Macaroons

2 large egg whites

¼ teaspoon salt

1 (14-ounce) can sweetened condensed milk

2 teaspoons vanilla extract

2 (14-ounce) bags shredded sweetened coconut

Apricot-almond dark chocolate macaroons

½ cup apricot jam

½–1 cup sliced almonds

½ cup dark chocolate chips

Piña colada macaroons

2 teaspoons rum extract, or to taste

½–1 cup dried sweetened pineapple, chopped

½–1 cup macadamia nuts, chopped

½ cup white chocolate chips

Red Corn Cookies

I love these corn cookies because they are part shortbread, part sugar cookie, and all delicious. They are sure to surprise anyone who tastes them because corn is an unusual ingredient in a cookie. I love adding a topping of lemon-lavender icing or hazelnut brittle—or both!—to bring the cookies to a new level. Enjoy with a big glass of milk! **Makes about 50 cookies**

Cookies

4 sticks (1 pound) unsalted butter, at room temperature

3 cups white sugar

2 large eggs

2⅔ cups all-purpose flour

½ cup Ramona Farms red corn flour

1⅓ cups Ramona Farms pima polenta or fine-ground cornmeal

1½ teaspoons baking powder

½ teaspoon baking soda

1 tablespoon kosher salt

Lemon-lavender icing (makes extra)

1 cup powdered sugar

2 teaspoons grated lemon zest

1 tablespoon lemon juice

1 tablespoon milk

1 small drop yellow food coloring (optional)

Leaves from 1 bunch lavender

Hazelnut brittle (makes extra)

4 cups white sugar

¼ teaspoon apple cider vinegar

1 cup water

5½ cups hazelnuts, finely chopped

1. Line a rimmed baking sheet with parchment paper. Combine the butter and sugar in the bowl of an electric mixer fitted with the paddle attachment and cream together on medium-high speed for 2–3 minutes. Scrape down the sides of the bowl, add the eggs, and beat for 7–8 minutes, until light and fluffy.

2. Reduce the mixer speed to low and add the all-purpose flour, corn flour, polenta, baking powder, baking soda, and salt. Mix just until the dough comes together, no longer than 1 minute. Scrape down the sides of the bowl.

3. For each cookie, scoop 2 tablespoons dough onto the prepared baking sheet. Pat the tops of the cookie dough domes flat. Wrap tightly in plastic wrap and freeze for 30 minutes. Meanwhile, preheat the oven to 350 degrees F.

4. Line a second rimmed baking sheet with parchment paper. Arrange the cookies 4 inches apart on both sheets (you will need to work in batches). Bake for 18 minutes, or until light golden brown on the edges. Let the cookies cool completely on the sheets. While the cookies are cooling, make the toppings.

5. For the lemon-lavender glaze, combine the powdered sugar, lemon zest and juice, milk, and food coloring (if using) in a medium bowl. Whisk vigorously until smooth. Using one sheet of cookies, dip half of each cookie in the icing. Sprinkle with the lavender.

6. For the hazelnut brittle, combine the sugar, vinegar, and water in a medium saucepan and cook over medium heat until the sugar dissolves. Continue cooking until the sugar turns a dark amber color, 20–22 minutes. Stir in the chopped nuts. Using the other sheet of cookies, dip half of each cookie into the hot caramel. Return the dipped cookies to the parchment-lined sheet until the caramel sets.

Malasadas Two Ways

If you've ever been to Hawai'i for Malasada Day, then you know how popular and delicious these pastries are. Hawaiian-style malasadas are a deep-fried Portuguese doughnut rolled in sugar, creating a light and fluffy treat that you can stuff with a creamy coconut haupia or guava pudding, or leave unfilled. It's the perfect dessert for all my sweet-tooth friends. **Makes about 25 malasadas**

1. In a small bowl, combine the yeast, warm water, and 2 teaspoons of the sugar. Set aside until foamy, about 10 minutes.

2. In the bowl of an electric mixer fitted with the paddle attachment, beat the eggs until light and fluffy. Add the whole milk, evaporated milk, melted butter, remaining 1 cup sugar, and yeast mixture and mix until well combined.

3. With the motor running, slowly add the flour and salt. Mix the dough until well combined and smooth, about 10 minutes.

4. Transfer the dough to a lightly greased bowl and cover with a clean towel. Place in a warm area and allow it to rise until doubled in size, at least 45 minutes or up to 2 hours.

5. Grease a rimmed baking sheet. Once the dough has risen, transfer it to a lightly floured surface. Roll or press the dough out to about 1 inch thick. Using a floured cookie cutter, cut 3-inch dough rounds. Place the dough rounds on the prepared baking sheet. Cover with a clean towel and allow to rest for at least 30 minutes.

6. Put some sugar in a large bowl and set aside. In a medium saucepan, heat about ½ inch of oil over medium-high heat to 375 degrees F. Set a wire rack over another rimmed baking sheet.

7. Working with a few dough rounds at a time, carefully lower the malasadas into the oil to fry. Do not crowd the malasadas. Fry until golden brown, 3–5 minutes on each side. Transfer the malasadas to the wire rack to cool slightly, then put them in the bowl of sugar and toss to coat evenly with sugar. Return the coated malasadas to the rack.

8. If you are stuffing your malasadas, put the haupia or guava filling (recipes follow) in a piping bag fitted with a metal tip. Push the tip into the side of the malasada and fill with the pudding.

2 tablespoons fast-acting instant yeast

¼ cup warm water (115°F)

2 teaspoons plus 1 cup sugar, plus more for coating

6 large eggs

1 cup whole milk

1 cup evaporated milk

4 tablespoons (½ stick) unsalted butter, melted

8 cups bread flour, plus more for dusting

½ teaspoon salt

Vegetable oil, for frying

Haupia Pudding filling or Guava Pudding filling (recipes follow)

(recipe continues)

★ Haupia Pudding ★

1 (13.5-ounce) can coconut milk
¼ cup sugar
2 tablespoons cornstarch
1 teaspoon vanilla extract

1. In a medium saucepan, combine the coconut milk, sugar, and cornstarch and heat over medium heat, stirring constantly. Cook until the mixture has thickened, 3–5 minutes.

2. Remove the pan from the heat and stir in the vanilla. Pour the filling into a bowl and cover with plastic wrap, pressing the plastic wrap down on the surface of the pudding to prevent a skin from forming. Refrigerate for at least 1 hour, until set. Keep chilled until ready to use.

★ Guava Pudding ★

1 cup whole milk
¼ cup plus 2 tablespoons sugar
3 large egg yolks
1 tablespoon cornstarch
⅛ teaspoon salt
¼ cup guava puree
1½ teaspoons unsalted butter
½ teaspoon vanilla extract

1. In a medium saucepan, combine the milk and 2 tablespoons of the sugar and bring to a simmer over medium-high heat.

2. In a medium bowl, whisk together the remaining ¼ cup sugar, egg yolks, cornstarch, and salt. Slowly add the heated milk to the yolk mixture, stirring constantly.

3. Return the mixture to the saucepan and cook, stirring constantly, until thickened, 2–3 minutes.

4. Remove from the heat and add the guava puree, butter, and vanilla. Whisk until smooth. Pour into a shallow dish and cover with plastic wrap, pressing the plastic wrap down on the surface of the pudding to prevent a skin from forming. Refrigerate for at least 1 hour, until set. Keep chilled until ready to use.

Manju Two Ways

Baking is where I feel most comfortable. One of my favorite baked goods is manju, a traditional Japanese steamed cake that's typically filled with red bean paste. We make them a little different here in Hawai'i. Buttery, flaky dough encases a coconut filling and is then baked to golden-brown perfection. **Makes 18 manju**

1. In a large bowl, whisk together the flour, sugar, and salt. Add the cold cubed butter and, using a pastry cutter, cut the butter in until the mixture is well combined and sandy in texture. Try to work quickly to keep the butter as cold as possible.

2. Add the milk and egg yolks. Mix until well combined and a ball of dough can be formed. Roll the dough into a log, wrap in plastic wrap, and refrigerate for at least 1 hour.

3. Meanwhile, make the filling(s). To make the anko filling, rinse the adzuki beans under cool running water until it runs clear. Put the adzuki beans and water in an Instant Pot. Close the lid and set to sealing. Cook on high pressure for 25 minutes. Allow 15 minutes natural pressure release. Drain the beans. Return the beans to the Instant Pot and set to sauté mode. Add the sugar and salt and cook, stirring, until the sugar dissolves and the beans have thickened. Use an immersion blender to blend until smooth. Set aside to cool slightly, then cover and transfer to the refrigerator until ready to use.

Dough

2⅔ cups all-purpose flour

2 tablespoons sugar

½ teaspoon salt

3 sticks (1½ cups) cold unsalted butter, cut into cubes

6 tablespoons milk

4 large egg yolks

Anko filling (makes extra)

1¼ cups dried adzuki beans

4 cups water

1 cup sugar

⅛ teaspoon salt

Coconut filling (makes extra)

1 cup coconut milk

1 cup unsweetened shredded coconut

½ cup sugar

Chocolate Sauce (recipe follows)

Egg wash

1 large egg

1 tablespoon water

(recipe continues)

4. To make the coconut filling, combine the coconut milk, shredded coconut, and sugar in a small saucepan. Cook over medium-high heat, stirring frequently, until most of the liquid has been absorbed. Remove from the heat and let cool slightly, then cover and transfer to the refrigerator until ready to use.

5. Preheat the oven to 350 degrees F. Line a rimmed baking sheet with parchment paper.

6. Cut the chilled dough log into 18 equal pieces. With your fingers, flatten each piece of dough into a 4-inch disk, keeping the center thicker than the edges. The edges should be about ¼ inch thick. Scoop about 1 tablespoon of either filling into the center of the dough.

7. Working with one disk at a time, bring the edges of the dough up toward the center. Pinch to seal the dough over the filling and smooth the seams together. Shape the dough into a ball with a slightly flattened top. Place the manju on the lined baking sheet, pinched seam side down.

8. Make the egg wash by whisking the egg and water together. Brush the tops of the manju with the egg wash.

9. Bake for 20–25 minutes, until golden brown. Let cool completely.

10. If making coconut manju, make the chocolate sauce while the cookies cool. Then drizzle the warm chocolate sauce on the coconut manju.

★ Chocolate Sauce ★

1 cup heavy cream
¾ cup semisweet chocolate chips
8 tablespoons (1 stick) unsalted butter
½ teaspoon vanilla extract

1. In a small saucepan, heat the cream over medium heat until it just begins to boil. Reduce the heat to low and add the chocolate chips. Stir until the chocolate chips have melted. Add the butter and vanilla and stir until smooth.

Knafeh Muffins

Baked Phyllo Cups

Knafeh (also spelled kanafa, kunafa, kanafeh, or knafe) is a wonderful shredded phyllo (kataifi) dessert that is common in much of the Middle East. My family would traditionally eat knafeh during the Jewish holiday of Shavuot, when it is customary to eat dairy foods. This dessert is that perfect combination of sweet, from the flavored syrup, and savory, from the gooey cheesy center. These mini knafeh are perfect bite-size snacks and a fun way to enjoy something that is more traditionally made as a larger cake. **Makes 24 mini knafeh**

1. Preheat the oven to 375 degrees F. Grease two 12-cup muffin tins.

2. Cut the kataifi into 1- or 2-inch strips and put in a bowl. Add the melted butter and salt. Using your hands, mix the kataifi and butter, tossing it to evenly coat the dough with the butter and break up any clumps.

3. Put about 1 tablespoon of the dough mixture in the bottom of each prepared muffin cup. Press the mixture down to form an even layer on the bottom.

4. In a separate bowl, combine the ricotta, mozzarella, and cardamom, stirring until evenly combined. Divide the ricotta mixture evenly on top of the dough mixture in the muffin cups, 1½–2 tablespoons per cup.

5. Divide the remaining kataifi dough evenly among the muffin cups and press the tops down firmly to cover the ricotta mixture and form a flat top.

6. Bake for about 30 minutes, until golden brown.

7. While the knafeh are baking, make the syrup. Combine the sugar, lemon juice, orange blossom or rose water, and water in a medium saucepan. Bring to a boil over medium heat, stirring constantly. Reduce the heat to a simmer and cook until it thickens, about 15 minutes. Allow to cool slightly.

8. Once the knafeh are done baking, remove them from the oven and pour the syrup evenly over each knafeh while still hot.

9. Garnish with rose petals, pistachios, and fennel pollen and serve warm.

Knafeh

1 (1-pound) package frozen kataifi (such as Apollo), thawed

1¾ cups (3½ sticks) unsalted butter, melted

2½ teaspoons salt

3 cups ricotta cheese

3 cups shredded mozzarella cheese

¼ teaspoon ground cardamom

3 cups sugar

1 tablespoon lemon juice

½ teaspoon orange blossom water or rose water

1 cup water

Garnishes

Dried rose petals

Chopped pistachios

Fennel pollen

Mithai

SALMAH

If there's one recipe that speaks to my family legacy, it's mithai. *Mithai* means sweet in Hindi, and it is most definitely a sweet! Anise-infused dough is fried and thickly coated with a cardamom syrup that crystallizes as it cools. My family's mithai recipe has been passed down for generations, and mithai making was traditionally a special event leading up to weddings. Family members would fly in days prior to make the dough, then fry, sugarcoat, and package the mithai—a mithai crew led by our family's matriarch to spearhead a massive batch of 20 or 30 pounds of confection, all in celebration of the bride and groom. **Makes about 20 mithai**

1. In a medium skillet, toast the anise seeds and cardamom seeds until fragrant. Let cool slightly, then grind in a coffee grinder. Transfer the ground spices to a large bowl. Add the flour and baking powder and whisk to combine.

2. In a small bowl, combine the melted ghee and butter. Slowly add the melted fats to the flour mixture, tossing the mixture and massaging the dough between your fingers for 7–10 minutes.

3. In another small bowl, whisk together the evaporated milk and egg. Slowly drizzle the milk and egg mixture into the flour mixture, about ½ cup at a time, continuing to toss the dough with your fingers.

4. Form the dough into a smooth ball, cover, and leave it to rest for 20 minutes at room temperature.

5. Meanwhile, in a large, heavy-bottomed pan, heat the oil over medium-high heat to 375 degrees F. Set a wire rack over a rimmed baking sheet. Line another rimmed baking sheet with parchment paper.

6. Transfer the dough to a floured surface and, using a rolling pin, roll the dough into a 1-inch-thick rectangle about 9 by 12 inches. Cut the dough into diamond shapes about 2 by 2 inches, or the desired size.

7. Once the frying oil is up to temperature, fry the diamond pieces a few at a time until they are a deep golden brown, 5–6 minutes, flipping the diamonds halfway through to brown both sides evenly. Transfer the diamonds to the wire rack to cool and drain.

8. To make the syrup, in a medium saucepan, combine the water, sugar, cardamom pods, and orange blossom water and bring to a soft boil over medium heat.

9. Working with a few pieces at a time, place the cooled mithai in a large bowl and slowly stream some of the sugar syrup over the fried pieces while vigorously turning the bowl and tossing to coat the mithai in the sticky syrup. Once nicely coated, set the mithai on the prepared baking sheet to dry.

Mithai

¼ cup anise seeds

Seeds from ¼ cup cardamom pods

3 cups all-purpose flour, plus more for dusting

5 teaspoons baking powder

¼ cup ghee, melted

4 tablespoons (½ stick) unsalted butter, melted

2 cups evaporated milk

1 large egg

4 cups vegetable oil

Sugar syrup

1½ cups water

2 cups sugar

4 cracked cardamom pods

2 teaspoons orange blossom water

Pine Tart and Cheese Roll

SALMAH

Pineapple tart (commonly called "pine tart") and a cheese roll rank among the top pastries in Guyana. They are legendary teatime treats: Buttery, flaky dough is filled with a spiced sweet pineapple jam and folded into petite triangles (for the pine tart) or filled with a spicy cheddar cheese paste and rolled into rectangles (for the cheese roll). My mom's were community favorites. When she baked them, my siblings and I would always fight to either brush on the egg wash or seal the edges with a fork.

You can use the same pastry to make the pine tart and the cheese roll. Each filling recipe here makes enough to fill all the dough, so if you want to make both, halve your filling ingredient amounts—or double up your pastry dough. **Makes 20–25 pastries**

Pastry dough

4 cups all-purpose flour, plus more for dusting

2 teaspoons white sugar

8 tablespoons (1 stick) cold unsalted butter

⅓ cup vegetable shortening

1 cup ice-cold water

Egg wash

2 large eggs

2 tablespoons water

Pineapple jam filling

1 (20-ounce) can crushed pineapple

1 teaspoon freshly grated nutmeg

1 cinnamon stick

1 whole clove

1 teaspoon vanilla extract

½ cup light brown sugar

¼ cup dark brown sugar

¼ cup white sugar

Cheese paste filling

12 ounces sharp cheddar cheese, grated

2 tablespoons Dijon mustard

1 teaspoon hot sauce

1 teaspoon garlic powder

1 teaspoon smoked paprika

1. To make the pastry dough, in a large bowl, whisk together the flour and sugar.

2. Grate the cold butter with a box grater. Add the grated butter and shortening to the flour mixture. Using a pastry cutter, cut the butter and shortening into the flour until it resembles coarse sand. Slowly add the ice-cold water, a couple of tablespoons at a time, working the water into the flour mixture with your hands. Gently knead the dough in the bowl to evenly incorporate the water.

3. Wrap the dough in plastic wrap and refrigerate for at least 1 hour, or until ready to use.

4. To make the pineapple jam, combine the pineapple, nutmeg, cinnamon, clove, vanilla, and sugars in a medium saucepan and stir to combine. Simmer over medium-low heat, stirring frequently to prevent burning, until the mixture thickens slightly into a jam-like consistency, 15–20 minutes. Remove the cinnamon stick and clove. Spread the jam in a shallow dish to cool. Refrigerate until ready to use.

(recipe continues)

5. To make the cheese filling, in a medium bowl, combine the shredded cheese, mustard, hot sauce, garlic powder, and smoked paprika. Stir until evenly combined. Refrigerate until ready to use.

6. Preheat the oven to 350 degrees F. Line a rimmed baking sheet with parchment paper.

7. Remove the pastry dough from the refrigerator and divide the dough in half. Rewrap half of the dough and return it to the refrigerator to use for the cheese rolls.

8. Make the egg wash by beating the eggs and water until well mixed.

9. If making the pineapple tarts, on a lightly floured surface, roll out the dough to ¼–⅛ inch thick. Cut the dough into circles using a 3-inch biscuit cutter. Cut as many circles as possible with the dough.

10. In the center of each circle, spoon 1–2 teaspoons pineapple jam, leaving room around the edge. Using a pastry brush, wet the edge of the circles with the egg wash.

11. Envisioning the three sides of a triangle, lift three sides of the circle of dough and pinch the edges to form a seam, forming a triangle with an opening in the center. If necessary, seal the three corners with a fork.

12. Place the pineapple tarts on the prepared baking sheet. Brush the dough edges with egg wash.

13. If making the cheese rolls, remove the remaining pastry dough from the refrigerator and place on a lightly floured surface. Roll out the dough to a rectangle ¼–⅛ inch thick. Using a bench scraper or knife, cut the dough into rectangles, about 3 × 4 inches.

14. Spoon 2 teaspoons cheese filling in a line down the middle of each dough rectangle, leaving room on the edges. Brush the dough edges with the egg wash.

15. Tightly roll the dough around the cheese filling, sealing the ends and the long edge with a fork. Pierce the top with a fork to release steam.

16. Place the cheese rolls on the prepared baking sheet. Brush the tops with egg wash.

17. Bake the pineapple tarts and/or cheese rolls for 25–30 minutes, until golden brown. Let cool before serving.

Triple Chocolate Cheesecake Cups

This recipe for *The Great American Recipe* Bake Sale challenge really hit home for me. Growing up in a Greek home, we were always very involved in our church. There always seemed to be a bake sale going on, and my mom, Nancy, was always the first to contribute. So this recipe is a tribute to her. Though I've made it many times over the years, especially for the holidays, the first time I made this was shortly before my mom lost her battle to cancer. She loved chocolate and absolutely loved this dessert: chocolate cheesecake with Oreo cookie crust and a chocolate ganache topping. I feel lucky that she had the chance to taste it before she passed. I used to make it as a full cheesecake, but it's particularly enjoyable made into cupcake-size personal cheesecakes. **Makes 24 cheesecake cups**

1. Preheat the oven to 350 degrees F. Line two 12-cup muffin tins with paper liners.

2. Pulverize the cookies in a food processor, grinding until evenly ground and sandy. Add the melted butter and pulse until it is thoroughly mixed in.

3. Divide the cookie crust mixture evenly among the lined muffin cups. Press the bottom of each one down firmly to compact the crust.

4. Bake for 5–8 minutes to set the crust. Set aside to cool. Lower the oven temperature to 325 degrees F.

5. Put the chocolate chips in a microwave-safe bowl and microwave until smooth, then let cool.

6. Meanwhile, in the bowl of an electric mixer fitted with the paddle attachment, beat the cream cheese until smooth. Add the sugar and sour cream and beat until smooth. Scrape the bowl and add the vanilla and eggs, beating well and scraping the bowl often to ensure there are no lumps.

7. Add the melted chocolate and mix thoroughly, scraping again to completely mix.

Chocolate cheesecake

¾ standard package chocolate sandwich cookies (such as Oreo, about 35 cookies)

8 tablespoons (1 stick) unsalted butter, melted

1 (12-ounce) package high-quality semisweet chocolate chips (such as Ghirardelli)

4 (8-ounce) packages cream cheese, softened

½ cup sugar

1 cup sour cream

2 teaspoons vanilla extract

4 large eggs, at room temperature

Sea salt to taste

Chocolate ganache

1½ cups high-quality semisweet chocolate chips (such as Ghirardelli)

½ cup heavy cream

(recipe continues)

8. Pour the batter onto the crusts in the muffin cups, leaving enough room at the top for the chocolate ganache.

9. Bake for 15–20 minutes, until the centers are just set.

10. While the cheesecakes are baking, make the chocolate ganache. Pour an inch or so of water into the bottom of a double boiler and bring to a simmer over medium heat. Combine the chocolate chips and cream in the top of the double boiler and place it on top. (If you don't have a double boiler, you can use any heat-safe bowl on top of a small saucepan; just make sure the bottom of the bowl doesn't touch the simmering water below.) Stir the chocolate as it melts until it is smooth. Remove from the heat and let cool. If needed, chill in the refrigerator for a little bit to help it set up.

11. When the cheesecakes are done baking, remove them from the oven and let cool to room temperature. Pour the ganache on top of each cheesecake and then chill to set.

12. To serve, sprinkle the tops with sea salt.

Fudgy Brownies Topped with Ganache

KHELA

This recipe combines several created by my friends and me. My friend JC taught me this fudgy brownie recipe that I keep in my back pocket for when I need it. My bestie Niki wowed me with how easy ganache was to make probably twenty years ago—and really, who doesn't love chocolate on their chocolate?! Finally, pecans are my favorite, and I'll put them on just about anything. I always have the roasted, salted pieces around, ready to throw in salads for the added crunch, to pulse for a breading, to snack on with some cheese, or to make into pralines, which I've been doing for as long as I can remember. This super quick and easy praline is a delicious topper for brownies. Of course, you can just toss some plain toasted pecans on top instead, and these brownies will still be amazingly delicious. **Makes 16 brownies**

1. Preheat the oven to 350 degrees F. Grease a 13 × 9-inch baking pan.

2. In a large saucepan, melt the butter over low heat, stirring occasionally. Add the dark chocolate and stir until melted and smooth. Remove the pan from the heat and let cool slightly.

3. In a large bowl, whisk together the eggs, buttermilk, oil, and vanilla. Add the sugars and whisk well. Add the melted chocolate mixture and whisk until smooth.

4. In a medium bowl, whisk together the flour, cocoa powder, and salt. Fold the dry ingredients into the chocolate mixture, mixing until well combined. Pour the batter into the prepared baking pan and bake for 25–30 minutes, rotating the pan halfway through, until a toothpick inserted in the center comes out clean. Set aside to cool.

5. To make the ganache topping, put the semisweet chocolate in a heat-proof bowl. Heat the cream in a small saucepan over high heat until it is simmering. As soon as it simmers, pour the cream over the chocolate, then cover the bowl and let it sit for several minutes. When removing the covering, take care not to let water droplets land in the ganache. After a few minutes, lightly stir the mixture with a whisk until the cream is incorporated and the ganache is smooth.

6. Spread the ganache evenly over the top of the cooled brownies. Sprinkle the top with the pecans and a touch of Maldon salt.

2 sticks (1 cup) unsalted butter

1 pound 70% dark chocolate chips

6 large eggs

½ cup buttermilk

½ cup olive oil

1 tablespoon vanilla extract

2 cups packed brown sugar

⅔ cup white sugar

1½ cups all-purpose flour

1½ cups cocoa powder

2 teaspoons kosher salt

1 (16-ounce) package semisweet chocolate chips

1 cup heavy cream

Easy-Peasy Sweet and Salty Pecans (recipe follows) or plain toasted pecans, for topping

Maldon salt, for finishing (optional)

(recipe continues)

★ Easy-Peasy Sweet and Salty Pecans ★

1 cup packed brown sugar

4 tablespoons (½ stick) unsalted butter

2 tablespoons water

2 cups roasted and salted pecan pieces

1. Combine the brown sugar, butter, and water in a large skillet and cook over high heat, stirring, until most of the water is gone, 2–3 minutes. Lower the heat to medium-high and let the sauce reduce for another minute. Stir in the pecan pieces and cook until all the pieces are nicely coated and begin to clump together, about 1 minute more. Spread them out in a single layer on a sheet of parchment paper and let cool completely.

Cinnamon Rolls with Cream Cheese Icing and Candied Pecans

LEANNA

Let me be clear. This recipe takes a little work and it is not quick. However, I think we can all agree that there is nothing quite like an ooey-gooey cinnamon roll fresh out of the oven. The smell that fills the house is simply unmatched. I may not have any scientific proof, but I believe that cinnamon rolls taste best when they are homemade. This is solely based on my own very unscientific study, but try this recipe out, and you can be the judge. **Makes 12 rolls**

1. In the bowl of an electric mixer fitted with the whisk attachment, whisk the egg, egg yolks, melted butter, brown sugar, and ¾ cup of the milk until smooth. Add 1¼ cups of the flour and whisk together until paste-like.

2. In a small microwave-safe bowl, warm the remaining ¾ cup milk to about 100 degrees F. Whisk the yeast into the milk and let sit for 5 minutes.

3. Add the salt to the dough in the mixer and whisk until thoroughly incorporated. Switch your mixer attachment from the whisk to the dough hook.

4. Add 2¼ cups more flour to the bowl and knead the dough on medium speed for 5–6 minutes. Add the yeast mixture and knead on low speed for another 5–6 minutes. If the dough is still sticky, add some flour a little at a time until the dough is moist and supple and forms a soft ball.

5. Transfer the dough ball to a lightly greased bowl, cover with a clean towel, and set aside to proof for 3–4 hours at room temperature. (It can also be left to rise overnight in the refrigerator.) The dough should be at least double its size.

6. Grease a 9 × 13-inch baking pan. Transfer the dough to a lightly floured surface. With floured hands, press the dough into a rectangle about 9 by 13 inches. If needed, re-flour your surface as you are stretching the dough to ensure that it does not stick.

7. For the topping, use a pastry brush to brush the melted butter onto the dough.

8. In a small bowl, combine the brown sugar and cinnamon and stir until well blended. Using your hands, spread the cinnamon sugar mix evenly onto the dough.

Rolls

1 large egg plus 4 large egg yolks, at room temperature (reserve 1 egg white for Candied Pecans)

6 tablespoons unsalted butter, melted

¼ cup packed brown sugar

1½ cups whole milk, divided

3½ cups all-purpose flour, divided, plus more for dusting

1 (¾-ounce) package active dry yeast

1¼ teaspoons kosher salt

Topping

1½ tablespoons unsalted butter, melted

1 cup packed brown sugar

1½ tablespoons ground cinnamon

Candied Pecans (recipe follows)

Cream cheese icing

½ cup (4 ounces) cream cheese

1½ cups powdered sugar

1 teaspoon vanilla extract

3 tablespoons whole milk

(recipe continues)

9. Starting with one of the 13-inch-long edges, roll the dough into a tight log. Using a bench scraper or knife, slice the log into 12 even slices, 1½ to 2 inches thick.

10. Place the cinnamon rolls cut side down in the prepared baking pan in three rows of four, spacing them evenly in the pan. Let the rolls rest in the pan for 20–30 minutes. Meanwhile, preheat the oven to 350 degrees F.

11. Bake for 25–30 minutes, until lightly golden on top.

12. While the cinnamon rolls are baking, make the cream cheese icing. Combine the cream cheese and powdered sugar in the bowl of an electric mixer fitted with the whisk attachment and whisk until smooth, starting with low speed to avoid a mess. Add the vanilla and milk and whisk until smooth.

13. Remove the cinnamon rolls from the oven and use a spatula to evenly spread the icing over them. Top with the candied pecans (below) and serve warm.

Nº 2 | Candied Pecans

1½ cups packed brown sugar
¼ cup white sugar
1 teaspoon sea salt
1 tablespoon ground cinnamon
½ teaspoon ground nutmeg
½ teaspoon ground ginger
1 large egg white
4 cups raw pecan halves

1. Preheat the oven to 300 degrees F. Line a rimmed baking sheet with parchment paper.

2. In a large bowl, combine the sugars, salt, cinnamon, nutmeg, and ginger.

3. In a medium bowl, whisk the egg white until it is light and frothy.

4. Add the pecans to the egg white and stir with a silicone spatula to get them fully coated in egg white.

5. Pour the pecans into the cinnamon-sugar mixture and stir until evenly coated.

6. Spread the pecans out on the prepared baking sheet. Bake for about 20 minutes, until they look dry. Let cool completely before using.

Liliko'i Bars and Strawberry Li Hing Mui Sauce with Macadamia Nut Brittle

RELLE

In this Hawaiian twist on lemon bars, sweet yet tangy liliko'i (passion fruit) curd is baked atop a delicious buttery shortbread crust and sprinkled with powdered sugar. Li hing mui is a Chinese salty dried plum. The literal Chinese translation is "traveling plum." It is made by pickling plum, licorice, red food coloring, sugar, and salt. You can find it in seed form or powder. It's a very popular flavor addition to snacks in Hawaii. This is the perfect dessert to share with your family and friends. **Makes 24 bars**

1. Preheat the oven to 350 degrees F. Grease a 9 × 13-inch baking pan with nonstick cooking spray.

2. To make the crust, in a large bowl, whisk together the flour, brown sugar, and salt. Add the cold cubed butter and, using a pastry cutter, cut the butter in until the mixture is well combined and sandy in texture.

3. Pour the crust mixture into the prepared pan and gently pat down to create an even crust layer. Bake for 15 minutes.

4. While the crust is baking, make the liliko'i curd. In a large bowl, whisk together the eggs, white sugar, and flour. Add the liliko'i juice and whisk again until well combined. Set aside.

5. Once the crust has finished parbaking, carefully pour the liliko'i mixture over the top. Return the pan to the oven and bake for another 30 minutes. The liliko'i curd will puff up and then sink down. Once it has sunk down and the edges have just begun to brown, it is done.

6. Cool completely, then cut into squares. Dust with the powdered sugar.

7. Meanwhile, to make the strawberry sauce, put the strawberries in a blender and blend until smooth. Transfer the pureed strawberries to a small saucepan and add the sugar and lemon juice. Cook over medium heat until the sauce thickens slightly, 5–10 minutes. Stir in the li hing mui powder.

8. Smear a spoonful of the sauce on each serving plate and place a liliko'i bar on top, along with a piece of macadamia nut brittle (recipe follows).

Crust

2 cups all-purpose flour

½ cup packed brown sugar

½ teaspoon salt

12 tablespoons (1½ sticks) cold unsalted butter, cut into cubes

Liliko'i curd

4 large eggs

1¼ cups white sugar

⅓ cup all-purpose flour

¾ cup liliko'i juice (passion fruit juice)

¼ cup powdered sugar

Strawberry sauce

8 ounces strawberries, hulled

2 tablespoons white sugar

1 teaspoon lemon juice

¼ teaspoon li hing mui powder

(recipe continues)

★ Macadamia Nut Brittle ★

2 tablespoons unsalted butter, divided
1 cup sugar
¼ cup water
¼ cup light corn syrup
1½ cups macadamia nuts, roughly chopped
¼ teaspoon baking soda
Sea salt to taste

1. Grease a rimmed baking sheet with 1 tablespoon of the butter.

2. In a large nonstick saucepan, combine the sugar, water, and corn syrup. Cook over medium-high heat, stirring occasionally, until golden brown, 4–6 minutes.

3. Add the macadamia nuts and continue cooking until the mixture turns a medium-brown color, 2–3 minutes. Remove from the heat, quickly add the baking soda and remaining 1 tablespoon butter, and stir carefully until completely incorporated. Quickly pour the brittle onto the prepared baking sheet, sprinkle with salt, and let cool.

4. Break the cooled brittle into pieces. Keep in an airtight container until ready to serve.

Cassava Pone

SALMAH

Finely grated cassava blended with shredded coconut, melded with condensed milk, and spiced with cinnamon, nutmeg, and black pepper is what makes pone. It is quite the laborious task to grate down the cassavas but well worth the effort. This gooey flourless cake is a specialty item in Guyanese bakeries and one of my all-time favorite Guyanese baked goods. The end pieces are where it's at! The crisped edges contrast delightfully with the gooey interior, making them an ideal go-with for a cup of tea. **Makes about 20 slices**

1. Preheat the oven to 350 degrees F. Grease 2 (9 × 9) baking pans or 1 (13 × 9) baking pan.

2. Finely grate the cassavas, either by hand with a box grater or in a food processor with a grating disk. (If you're using a food processor, you may need to cut the cassavas into pieces to fit the food processor tube.)

3. With a clean tea towel, squeeze the excess liquid from the grated cassava and transfer it to a bowl. Add the shredded coconut, condensed milk, coconut milk, cinnamon, nutmeg, pepper, and salt, and stir to combine.

4. In a separate medium bowl, whisk together the eggs, evaporated milk, and sugars until well blended.

5. Slowly stream the egg mixture into the cassava mixture and stir to combine.

6. Pour the batter into the prepared baking dish(es) and spread it out evenly with a rubber spatula.

7. Bake until the edges are set and golden and a toothpick inserted in the center comes out clean, 25–30 minutes. Let the pone cool and set for 10 minutes before slicing.

3 medium to large cassavas (about 4 pounds), peeled and cut into thirds

2 cups finely shredded grated coconut

1 (14-ounce) can sweetened condensed milk

1 (14-ounce) can coconut milk

3 tablespoons ground cinnamon

1 tablespoon freshly grated nutmeg

2 teaspoons freshly cracked black pepper

1 teaspoon salt

3 large eggs

1 (12-ounce) can evaporated milk

½ cup white sugar

½ cup packed light brown sugar

Halwa

Halwa is a soft, decadently sweet treat that initiates conversation, and in the Guyanese community it is made to mark momentous occasions. From engagements to birthdays to birth announcements to home purchases, halwa is made to celebrate! When I was growing up, we also had halwa after Jumma, or Friday prayer service. To make it, flour is cooked into butter, smoothed with a spiced milk syrup, and dotted with raisins and cherries. **Serves 12–15**

SALMAH

1 cup whole milk

1 cup sugar

2 cinnamon sticks

6 whole cloves

2 sticks (1 cup) unsalted butter

1 cup all-purpose flour

1 (12-ounce) can evaporated milk

¼ cup maraschino cherries, chopped

¼ cup raisins

1. In a medium saucepan, combine the whole milk, sugar, cinnamon, and cloves and bring to a boil over medium-high heat.

2. Meanwhile, melt the butter in a large, heavy-bottomed saucepan over medium heat. Add the flour and cook, stirring constantly. The mixture will become runny and smooth and will start to take on color. After about 8 minutes, the mixture will be toasted and start to crumble and become slightly broken looking.

3. Strain the milk mixture and slowly add it to the flour mixture, a little at a time and mixing constantly. Only add more once the first small amount is fully incorporated.

4. Once all of the milk mixture has been added, remove the pan from the heat and add the evaporated milk. Stir until fully incorporated and smooth. Stir in the cherries and raisins.

5. Scoop or pipe the halwa into individual bowls or cups and serve.

Tembleque

Coconut Pudding

ALEJANDRA

I think there has never been a more perfectly named dessert than tembleque, which gets its name from the Spanish word for "tremble," referring to the wiggly-jiggly texture of this molded coconut pudding. This Puerto Rican classic is enjoyed year-round and can often be found at bakery and dessert shops around the island. It's a childhood favorite of mine that still gives me great joy. I have fond memories of begging my dad to buy me some anytime I saw it at the dessert counter. Fortunately, I never had to beg too hard as he's also very much a fan of the creamy coconut treat. Made with just a few ingredients, the dessert is naturally vegan and gluten-free and can be made in advance, which makes it an ideal fuss-free dessert for entertaining—something that grown-up me extremely appreciates! **Serves 8**

1. Grease eight 4-ounce molds or one 8- or 9-inch baking pan (you can use ramekins, baking pans, or custard cups; nonstick baking molds tend to work best) with a small spritz of nonstick cooking spray or coconut oil.

2. In a medium saucepan over medium-high heat, combine the coconut milk, salt, and sugar, stirring until the sugar is dissolved.

3. Remove 1 cup of the warm coconut milk to a bowl, add the cornstarch, and whisk to create a smooth slurry. Slowly whisk the mixture back into the pan. Let the mixture cook, whisking constantly, until thickened and pudding-like, 3–5 minutes.

4. Remove from the heat. Divide the pudding into the prepared molds and let cool on the counter for 20 minutes, then loosely cover with plastic wrap and refrigerate for at least 4 hours, until set.

5. You can serve the tembleque in the ramekins, or run a thin wet knife around the edge of each ramekin and carefully invert onto a plate. (If using a baking pan, cut the tembleque into squares.)

6. Garnish the top with a sprinkle of ground cinnamon just before serving.

4 cups canned coconut milk (full-fat, please!)

½ teaspoon kosher salt

⅔ cup sugar

½ cup cornstarch

Ground cinnamon, for garnish

Rum and Raisin Bread Pudding

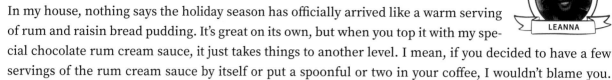

LEANNA

In my house, nothing says the holiday season has officially arrived like a warm serving of rum and raisin bread pudding. It's great on its own, but when you top it with my special chocolate rum cream sauce, it just takes things to another level. I mean, if you decided to have a few servings of the rum cream sauce by itself or put a spoonful or two in your coffee, I wouldn't blame you.

Serves 6–9

Bread pudding

3 large eggs, at room temperature

¾ cup sugar

1 cup heavy cream

1 cup whole milk

1 teaspoon ground cinnamon

½ teaspoon ground nutmeg

1 tablespoon vanilla bean paste

¼ cup rum cream liqueur

4 ounces stale French bread (about ½ loaf), cut into bite-size pieces

½ cup raisins

Chocolate rum cream sauce

3 tablespoons sweetened condensed milk

¼ cup rum cream liqueur

¼ cup chocolate liqueur

1. In the bowl of an electric mixer fitted with the whisk attachment, whisk the eggs and sugar on low speed until a creamy yellow paste forms. Add the cream, milk, cinnamon, nutmeg, and vanilla paste and whisk thoroughly. Whisk the rum into the mixture.

2. Add the bread pieces to the milk mixture and stir until the bread is fully coated. Refrigerate the bread pudding mixture for about 40 minutes to allow the bread to soak up all the liquid.

3. Meanwhile, preheat the oven to 350 degrees F. Generously butter 6 ramekins. (Alternatively, an 8-inch square cake pan can be used.)

4. Remove the bread pudding mixture from the refrigerator and stir in the raisins. Fill the ramekins with the mixture.

5. Place the ramekins in a large casserole dish and fill the casserole dish about one-third of the way up with water, creating a water bath for the bread puddings. Carefully place the casserole dish in the oven. Bake for about 45 minutes, until the centers are set up.

6. When the bread pudding has about 10 minutes remaining to bake, make the chocolate rum cream sauce. In a medium saucepan, whisk together the sweetened condensed milk, rum cream liqueur, and chocolate liqueur. Allow the sauce to bubble over medium heat, then remove it from the heat. Keep warm until ready to serve.

7. Remove the bread puddings from the oven. If a cake pan was used, cut into 9 squares and set on plates. Smother each square or ramekin with chocolate rum cream sauce.

Guyanese Plait Bread

SALMAH

There is no smell like freshly baked bread! I have vivid memories of growing up in Richmond Hill, waiting for the early morning train on Liberty Avenue, which was lined with Guyanese bakeries, all with the aroma of baked bread wafting through the streets. There's a mellow, soft sweetness to warm bread, and you can scarf down an entire loaf almost before you realize. A plain braided loaf, with a thin plait showing on the top, is what makes Guyanese bread distinctive. Guyanese are simple people, and descriptors enhance a dish's name. **Makes 1 large loaf**

1. In the bowl of an electric mixer, stir together the water and sugar, then sprinkle the yeast over the mixture and let it rest for 10 minutes. The yeast should become foamy and bubbly.

2. Add the flour, melted butter, and salt to the yeast mixture and, using the dough hook attachment, begin combining to form the dough. Continue to knead for 8–10 minutes to create a sticky dough. (Alternatively, you can knead the dough by hand using a wooden spoon.)

3. Transfer the dough to a lightly greased bowl and cover with a clean towel. Leave it to proof for 45 minutes, or until it has doubled in size.

4. Transfer the dough to a lightly floured surface. Gently roll the dough into a log and separate it into three equal parts. Roll each part into a long rope at least 12 inches long; make the ropes equal in length. Take an end of each of the ropes and pinch them together. Braid the three ropes by taking the alternating outside pieces and placing it in between the other two pieces. Finish by pressing together the ends and tucking both ends under to create clean ends to the loaf.

5. Lightly grease a rimmed baking sheet. Place the braided bread on the prepared sheet and allow it to rise for 25 minutes. Meanwhile, preheat the oven to 350 degrees F.

6. Bake the loaf for 30 minutes, or until it is a deep golden brown. Remove the loaf from the oven and immediately brush with melted butter.

1¼ cups warm water (100–105°F)

¼ cup sugar

2 envelopes (4½ teaspoons) fast-acting instant yeast

3½ cups all-purpose flour, plus more for dusting

4 tablespoons (½ stick) unsalted butter, melted, plus more for brushing

1 teaspoon salt

Sweet Coconut Bread with Sorrel

LEANNA

Sweet bread is a Bajan delicacy. It's packed with mixed citrus peel and spiced coconut and is the perfect complement to a hot cup of tea (with a splash of evaporated milk, which is my favorite way to have tea). Whether you are going through the everyday hustle and bustle or taking a pause to celebrate a major milestone, sweet bread is the perfect treat. I've watched my mother make sweet bread for over thirty years now and I like to think that I've mastered making it the way she does. The smell alone brings me tremendous joy, and it is my sincere hope that this recipe brings joy to your kitchen too.

Sorrel is the Caribbean name for hibiscus or roselle—not to be confused with the leafy greens called sorrel in the US. If you are looking for dried hibiscus in international markets, it may be labeled dried sorrel. **Makes 2 loaves**

7 cups all-purpose flour, plus more for dusting

1½ cups packed brown sugar

2 tablespoons baking powder

1 teaspoon salt

2 large eggs

2 sticks (1 cup) unsalted butter, melted

¾ cup whole milk

¾ cup coconut water

3 teaspoons vanilla extract, divided

1 cup mixed candied citrus peel

1 cup raisins

3 (7-ounce) bags unsweetened shredded coconut, divided

2 teaspoons ground nutmeg

1 tablespoon ground cinnamon

1 tablespoon almond extract

Maraschino cherries, for garnish

White sugar, for sprinkling

1. Preheat the oven to 325 degrees F. Grease two 9 × 5-inch loaf pans.

2. In a large bowl, whisk together the flour, brown sugar, baking powder, and salt.

3. In a medium bowl, whisk together the eggs, melted butter, milk, coconut water, and 2 teaspoons of the vanilla.

4. Add the wet ingredients to the dry ingredients and stir until a soft dough forms. Add the citrus peel, raisins, and 1 cup of the shredded coconut. Mix the ingredients until well incorporated.

5. Transfer the dough to a lightly floured surface and knead lightly. Divide the dough into two equal parts. Working with one half at a time, press and shape the dough until it forms a loaf. Place the loaves in the prepared pans.

6. In a large bowl, combine the remaining shredded coconut, nutmeg, cinnamon, almond extract, and remaining 1 teaspoon vanilla.

7. Split each loaf in half down its center line, being careful not to cut all the way through to the bottom. Stuff both loaves with the coconut mixture, then pinch the opening closed and smooth out the tops as much as possible with your fingers. There will be extra coconut filling; reserve for future use.

(recipe continues)

8. Using a sharp knife, carefully carve a diamond shape pattern on the top of each loaf. Place a maraschino cherry in the center of some of the diamonds, but not all. Sprinkle the top with white sugar.

9. Bake the loaves for 60–70 minutes, until deep golden brown. Let the loaves cool slightly, then remove from their pans and slice. Serve with sorrel (below).

№ 2 | Sorrel

1 gallon water

4½ ounces dried hibiscus

3 cinnamon sticks

Strips of peel from 1 orange

3 cups brown sugar, or to taste

1 tablespoon ground ginger

¼ teaspoon ground cloves

1. In a large saucepan, bring the water to a boil over high heat. Add the dried hibiscus, cinnamon sticks, and orange peel, reduce the heat, and simmer for 3–4 minutes. Remove the pan from the heat, cover, and let sit and steep overnight.

2. Strain the tea into a large bowl or pitcher. Stir in the brown sugar, ginger, and cloves. Continue to stir until the sugar dissolves.

3. Taste the tea and add more brown sugar if desired. Serve hot or over ice.

Fig Upside–Down Cake with Whipped Cream

BRAD

This upside-down cake is simply divine. Fresh figs, caramel, a moist buttermilk batter, and a subtle flavoring of rose water—it's a winning combination and a sure crowd-pleaser. It's also relatively easy to make, so it's great for those nonbakers who want to impress their company with a delicious and impressive-looking dessert. **Serves 8–10**

1. Preheat the oven to 350 degrees F. Grease a 9-inch round cake pan and line with parchment paper.

2. Arrange the fig halves, cut side down, in a pattern in the prepared cake pan.

3. In a small saucepan, combine the white sugar and water and cook over medium-high heat until caramelized, 4–6 minutes. Do not stir the caramel, but shake or swirl the pan if needed. Once the caramel is a nice amber color, carefully pour it over the figs in the pan. Set aside.

4. In a separate saucepan, melt the butter over medium heat. Cook, stirring frequently, until the butter takes on a golden-brown color and solid bits start to appear, about 5 minutes. Carefully pour the melted butter into a heat-safe bowl and set it aside to cool slightly.

5. In a large bowl, whisk together the flour, brown sugar, baking powder, baking soda, salt, cinnamon, and cardamom until evenly mixed.

12 fresh figs, halved

¾ cup white sugar

3 tablespoons water

2 sticks (1 cup) unsalted butter

2 cups all-purpose flour

½ cup packed brown sugar

½ teaspoon baking powder

½ teaspoon baking soda

½ teaspoon salt

1 teaspoon ground cinnamon

½ teaspoon ground cardamom

2 large eggs

1 cup honey

¾ cup buttermilk

Grated zest and juice of 1 lemon

1 teaspoon vanilla extract

1 teaspoon rose water

Garnishes

Honey

Fresh figs

Sliced almonds

Grated lemon zest

(recipe continues)

6. In a separate bowl, whisk together the eggs, honey, buttermilk, cooled browned butter, lemon zest and juice, vanilla, and rose water until thoroughly combined.

7. Add the wet ingredients to the dry ingredients and whisk until mostly smooth (a few small lumps are OK). Pour the batter over the figs and caramel in the pan.

8. Bake the cake for 45–55 minutes, until the top is deep golden brown and the center springs back to the touch. Set aside to cool.

9. Invert the cake onto a serving dish. Carefully remove the parchment paper. Drizzle the top with honey and garnish with fresh figs, sliced almonds, and lemon zest. Serve with whipped cream (below).

★ Whipped Cream ★

1 cup cold heavy cream
¼ cup crème fraîche
3 tablespoons powdered sugar
1 teaspoon vanilla extract

1. In an electric mixer fitted with the whisk attachment, whip the cream to soft peaks. Add the crème fraîche, powdered sugar, and vanilla and whip to stiff peaks. Chill until ready to serve.

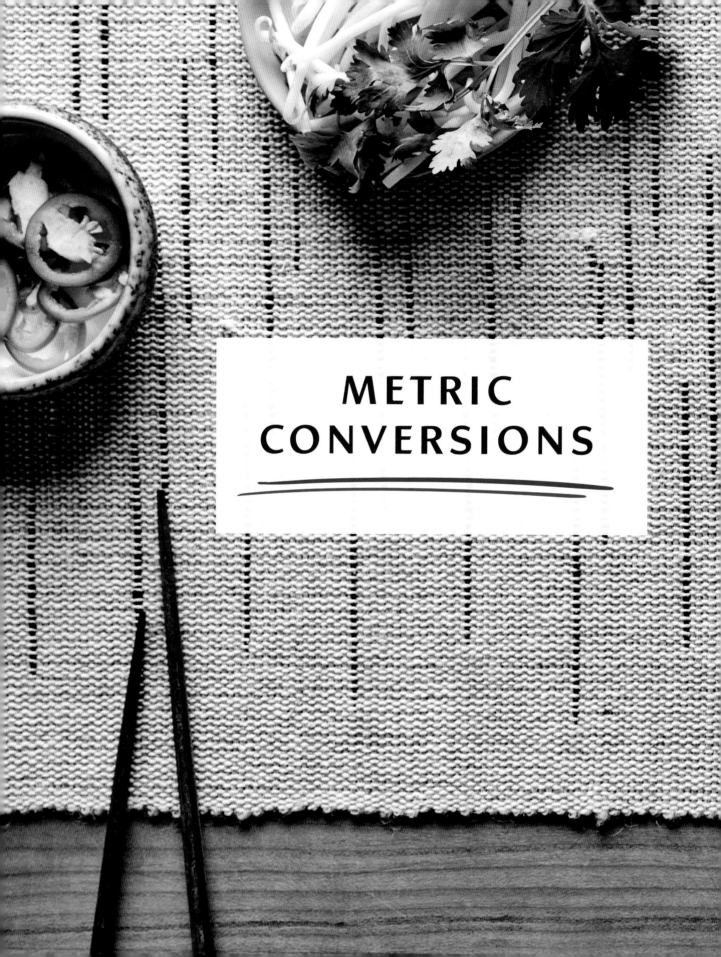

METRIC
CONVERSIONS

U.S. STANDARD		U.K.
¼ teaspoon	▷	¼ teaspoon (scant)
½ teaspoon	▷	½ teaspoon (scant)
¾ teaspoon	▷	½ teaspoon (rounded)
1 teaspoon	▷	¾ teaspoon (slightly rounded)
1 tablespoon	▷	2½ teaspoons
¼ cup	▷	¼ cup minus 1 dessert spoon
⅓ cup	▷	¼ cup plus 1 teaspoon
½ cup	▷	⅓ cup plus 2 dessert spoons
⅔ cup	▷	½ cup plus 1 tablespoon
¾ cup	▷	½ cup plus 2 tablespoons
1 cup	▷	¾ cup plus 2 dessert spoons

INDEX